D0949869

LORD, I NEED A MIRACLE

LORD, I NEED A MIRACLE

From the

Author of

Good Morning

Holy

Spirit

BENNY HINN

Publishers Since 1798

THOMAS NELSON PUBLISHERS
NASHVILLE

Published in Nashville, Tennessee, by Thomas Nelson, Inc.
Unless otherwise noted, Scripture quotations are from the NEW KING JAMES VERSION of the Bible. Copyright © 1979, 1980, 1982, Thomas Nelson, Inc., Publishers. Printed in the United States of America.

Scripture quotations noted KJV are from the KING JAMES VERSION of the Bible.

ISBN 0-8407-6251-8 (hard)

Printed in the United States of America

Contents

Contents

FOREWORD

———— ✝ ————

I do not understand why some people are healed and others are not. That is a mystery that will remain until the Lord returns. Benny Hinn is a man with an extraordinary gift at encouraging other people's faith, and he also has a very unique anointing of the Holy Spirit. He would be the first to tell you that he can heal no one, but it is through the power of the Holy Spirit that people are healed.

The viability of the medical files I have reviewed on each of the stories included in this book are extremely impressive. David Lane, in particular, with the diagnosis of adenocarcinoma of the rectum which was proven by rectal biopsy, was found to be free of all cancer when he went in for an emergency appendectomy. This information is documented by Mr. Lane's colorectal surgeon. I have talked at length with Mr. Lane regarding his testimony and reviewing the medical reports concerning him and am overwhelmed in how the Lord took a man with less than thirty days to live and performed a great miracle.

I have also personally talked with Marsha Brantley

who was suffering from lupus, Raynaud's, Sjögren's and ankylosing spondylitis. Mrs. Brantley related to me the many years of pain and suffering that she experienced due to her lupus and other ailments. Since she received her dramatic healing on October 18, 1991, through the word of knowledge at the Benny Hinn crusade, her medical doctor documented that her physical exam was normal except for some increased pigmentation which was a result of one of the medicines she had taken. This is quite a dramatic healing since lupus is medically an incurable disease. After talking at length with both Mr. and Mrs. Brantley and discussing the many signs and symptoms of her diseases, it is truly a miracle to see this lady standing totally transformed by the power of God.

The other miracles that you will read in this book are carefully documented by the patient's physicians and each testimony documents a dramatic change in the patient's condition. This dramatic change in their conditions can only be explained as a miraculous touch from God.

This book will certainly inspire one's faith to believe God for their miracle. With God, all things are possible to him who believes. In the testimonies that follow I believe that your faith will soar as the Holy Spirit encourages you to believe in miracles.

DONALD COLBERT, M.D.
December, 1992

Part One

The Miracles Needed

Chapter 1

†

"You've Got Thirty Days"

"You have two choices," the doctor told Dave Lane. "If we do the surgery now, you will survive about three months. Without it, you've got thirty days to live."

Those words came as a total shock. At nearly six feet tall, with dark black hair and a black beard, Dave was the picture of health. He was forty-one years old, but felt like twenty. "I loved life more than anything," he said.

It was the summer of 1990. Dave Lane and his wife, Rebecca, had spent more than a decade developing a successful Arabian horse farm near Cookeville, Tennessee. Their farm is home to "Muscats," a well-known champion stallion, and over twenty purebred Arabian horses.

Then one day Dave's body began telling him that something was not right. "I felt an unusual swelling in my stomach. There was a lot of pain. And I was passing blood."

"It Doesn't Look Good"

On Friday, June 15, 1990, he made an appointment to see his doctor. The examination did not last long. Immediately, the physician said, "Mr. Lane, I need to call the hospital and schedule more extensive tests. I'd like to do it right now."

Dave Lane will never forget that day. "When we got to the hospital my physician introduced me to a surgeon, and they prepared me for a complete examination of my colon."

"Mr. Lane," one of the doctors told him, "it doesn't look good."

The physicians found a tumor so large they could not get past it to examine the rest of the lower colon. They rushed the biopsy through the lab. The results confirmed their greatest fear. On his surgical pathology report the final diagnosis read: "Large mass (biopsy); Adenocarcinoma of Colon." That's the technical name for a malignant tumor.

Says Dave, "They expressed their concern about the considerable size of the cancerous growth and the length of time it had been there."

The tumor the doctors found was a little larger than a baseball. What they *hadn't* found concerned them even more. They had to be honest with Dave and explain that there could be additional tumors past the blockage, in areas they could not see.

It was Friday and one of the physicians had planned to be out of the city that weekend. But he was ready to rearrange his schedule because of the urgency of the situation. "We need to remove the tumor as soon as possible," the doctor told Dave.

More Bad News

After discussing the matter with the physicians, Dave decided he should make an appointment with another doctor to get a second opinion.

That's what he did, but the prognosis was the same. He even went to a *third* clinic and received the same dreadful news.

Says Dave, "I was told that if I did nothing about the cancer it would invade other vital organs of my body." The doctors were especially concerned about it spreading to his liver and causing cell reproduction to stop.

The more Dave talked with physicians, the more distressed he became. He learned that because of the extensive surgery he was facing, and the tumor's possible involvement with his spine, he could be paralyzed from the waist down. He was also told that he would likely lose all bowel and bladder functions.

The prognosis was poor, and he was completely overwhelmed by what he faced.

"One day I visited my doctor with what I considered a minor problem, and I was told the awful truth that I had cancer and was going to die," he said.

The words of the doctor kept ringing in his ears. "You've got thirty days to live. You've got thirty days to live."

"No Surgery for Me"

At home, Dave told his wife, Rebecca, "Honey, the doctors say I'm going to die with or without the surgery. I have decided not to have it."

Instead, he made plans to spend the last days of his life with his family. He began the task of getting his personal affairs in order.

The doctor became concerned at Dave's reluctance to discuss the situation. So he wrote his patient a letter.

"Dear Mr. Lane: I have tried to call you on several occasions, but you have been out of town or unavailable. I understand from talking to your son that you have not had anything done about the cancer in your rectum and I would urge you most strongly to have this problem dealt with as soon as possible. Cancer of the rectum is a serious, potentially fatal disease if left untreated, and you can expect it to spread to other parts of the body if it is not removed. If it is left unattended and spreads, then it is unlikely that you will recover," the doctor wrote.

To Dave Lane, there was only one hope for survival. It was something he was certain the physicians and surgeons would never understand.

Early in his life, Dave had become a Christian. He was active in his church. For the past year Dave had been serving God faithfully in a prison ministry. As a result of their meetings in local jails and area penitentiaries, he had seen scores of inmates transformed by the power of God.

The church in which Dave was raised, however, believed that God's power to heal was limited to New Testament times. But the more he read the Word, the more convinced he became that the Lord is the same "yesterday, today, and forever."

Now, there was nowhere else to turn. The doctors had pronounced a death sentence.

"Lord," he prayed, "I need a miracle."

Chapter 2

---✝---

Kathie's Environmental Attacks

On May 19, 1980, Mount St. Helens erupted in the state of Washington. It spewed enormous volumes of ash, darkened the skies, and polluted the environment for hundreds of miles.

Kathie McGahuey remembers it well. At the age of thirty-three, she lived with her husband and children in Milwaukie, Oregon, a suburb of Portland.

Kathie doesn't blame her problems on the volcano, but she marks that date as the time she began to know that something was drastically wrong. "All of a sudden when I would eat, I would get very ill," she said.

A Life-Threatening Reaction

Nothing like this had happened before. "Oh, we all have things that make us itch and scratch as children, but my health had been basically good all of my life," recalls Kathie.

The reactions became worse. She was rushed to the hospital by ambulance four different times. "My family thought I was having a heart attack," Kathie recalls.

By the time she reached the emergency room, the symptoms were subsiding, and the doctors found it impossible to diagnose or document her condition. Finally, the fourth time she had one of her unusual attacks, the reaction was severe enough that the physicians were able to diagnose her problem through testing her blood and monitoring her heart. Kathie was told she had "anaphylactic shock," a rare, severe, frightening, and life-threatening allergic reaction.

In most people this reaction occurs most commonly after an insect sting or in response to a particular drug like penicillin. In Kathie's case, the doctors had no idea of the underlying cause.

The McGahuey's family physician, a general practitioner who had seen her since childhood, did not know which way to turn. "He was a wonderful doctor, and I will never forget the day he wept with me because of my condition," says Kathie.

She was referred to an outstanding allergist, but because so many antidotes caused a severe reaction he was extremely cautious. He was fearful she would die from the tests. It seemed that almost everything the doctor tried made her condition worse because (as he would later learn) of the dyes and the chemicals. "I was told I am a universal reactor; I am allergic to almost every stimulus," she says.

Years of Frustration

For the next several years Kathie, her family, and her doctors worked diligently to find an answer. It was a matter of trial and error as they searched for the cause of her Type I hypersensitive reaction. Was it tree pollen? House dust? Yeast? Specific foods? They tried gradually increasing the doses of various allergens to promote the formation of antibodies to block certain reactions.

Nothing worked. After countless tests, the medical community was still puzzled about the cause of her symptoms. One allergist said, "Kathie, you are the one-in-a-hundred that we cannot help."

On some days, following an attack, she would have huge lumps in her throat. Says Kathie, "My throat would slam shut, and I would have that terrible reaction that causes the muscles around your heart to spasm. I also experienced severe oxygen loss to my brain. I would simply black out."

Kathie became confused and discouraged about her condition. "If it was caused by something I was eating, why couldn't they tell me?" she wondered. "I simply didn't understand."

Later she learned that part of what she was reacting to was not necessarily the food, but what was *on* the food. But that was only a part of her problem.

In documenting her condition, one of her doctors wrote, "This patient has suffered from extreme environmental illness, or chemical hypersensitivity syndrome for several years. She had anaphylactic reactions after exposure to certain substances and has required emergency hospitalization on numerous occasions."

The report continued: "She has had food allergies and sensitivities so extreme that her diet was reduced to potatoes (all other food caused a reaction). She could not tolerate soaps, detergents, perfume smells, synthetic clothing, vinyl, city tap water, diesel smoke, and numerous other allergens. There were residues of viruses in her system from previous illnesses that her weakened immune system could not eradicate which led to flare-ups in various organs."

Living in a Controlled Environment

With no solution to her problem, in 1985 Kathie McGahuey had what can only be described as a total metabolic breakdown. "When most of my vital organs—liver, kidneys, spleen, and adrenal glands—began to shut down," she said, "the doctors believed I was dying."

Her condition became so severe that her skin peeled off in sheets from head to toe. "I was like a snake shedding its skin," she says. "People would see me and turn their heads. AIDS was becoming a household word during this time and people were obviously thinking the worst."

The trauma Kathie was experiencing was equally difficult for her husband, Kenneth, who was pained to see her in this condition. "At first he didn't understand and wanted to run from the reality of it," she says. "But as my problems grew more critical, he became a tower of strength."

As time progressed, Kathie became reclusive. She learned that if she controlled her environment, the reactions would not be as frequent. "I literally had to lock myself in and stay away from the things that I felt would bother me."

Any work she did was confined to the home. "I had to learn that I could not live like the rest of the world," she said.

"People don't understand what it is like to be in a location where there are cleaning chemicals, food and other odors," says Kathie. "It's like the entire environment attacks you. Everything you smell, or touch, or eat, makes you sick. It would be easier to die than to live."

"Will I Ever Be Healed?"

There was one public place she did go—her church. Since the day she gave her heart to Christ at the age of eight, the Lord had been at the center of her life.

The people in the congregation were deeply concerned about her problem and did everything possible to create a healthy environment. "They were a wonderful group of people who provided tremendous emotional and spiritual support," she says.

Her friends watched Kathie's condition go back and forth like a pendulum. "They saw me become gauntly thin and then all of a sudden swell up because of an attack of gout."

Three different times Kathie lost her hair. "It was as if my body was going through chemotherapy," she explains. When her hair did grow back, it was totally gray.

As a Christian, Kathie believed that it was not God's will for her to die, but she admitted, "It would have been easier for me to die than to live. It's difficult when you have been battling an illness for so many years."

Kathie McGahuey is a woman of faith, but it was difficult for her to continue to say, "By Jesus' stripes I am healed" and have other people look at her and say, "There must be something wrong. It's taking too long."

Kathie wondered, "Will the Lord ever answer my prayer? Will I ever be healed?"

Chapter 3

✝

Forever Blind?

For over two years, Lynn Whitmore suffered with migraine headaches. "The pain was almost unbearable," she recalls. "And they were becoming more frequent and severe."

Lynn had lived in east Tennessee for only three years and didn't know where to turn. She had a college degree in music and planned a career as a concert performer.

In 1989 Lynn was admitted to the East Tennessee Baptist Hospital in Knoxville for extensive tests.

While she was lying in her hospital bed with another of her terrible headaches, she suddenly called out to the nurse on duty. "Please get a doctor," she cried. "I just went blind in my right eye."

The doctor came immediately, and he checked the platelets and the disks in the eye. The disks in the right eye were swollen and puffy, indicating excessive pressure on the optic nerve. He also knew that serious damage was taking place.

"I Had No Vision at All"

Lynn was diagnosed as having what is known as *pseudotumor cerebri*, a condition which causes the brain to feel there is a tumor or other object in the body that does not belong there. The body combats the condition by creating spinal fluid pressure. In Lynn's case, the force was three times what it should have been.

The pressure was on the optic nerve that goes to the eye. As the doctors explained it, the body was trying to get rid of something it felt was there. In the process, it was creating a far greater problem.

"They rushed me into surgery and put a lumbar shunt in the lower spinal cord to relieve the pressure and to keep me from losing my sight in the other eye," says Lynn.

She had hoped that her sight would return after the operation, but she still could not see anything with her right eye. "Even with a bright light shining in my eye I had no vision at all," says Lynn.

The shunt, she soon learned, was unsuccessful.

The doctors explained to her it was not the eye itself that had been damaged. The damage was in the optic tract connected to the brain. Actually there are two separate optic tracts, one for the left eye and one for the right.

In Lynn's case, the pressure on one of the tracts was so great that it was destroyed and she lost her vision. Then came the saddest news of all. "I was told by the doctor that the damage was irreversible," said Lynn, shaking her head.

The tract will not regenerate.

A Laundry List of Medical Problems

After the surgery, she continued to have intense headaches. Lynn told the physician, "I don't know if I can handle the torment my body is going through."

"We don't have many options," he told her. "You may have to learn to live with the pain."

Lynn slowly began to lose the vision in her other eye. "I felt so helpless," she recalls.

Her physician wrote in her medical report: "Yesterday she had the onset of facial twitching. She has undergone a lumboperitoneal shunt. She suffers from persistent headaches. She also has visual loss secondary to pseudotumor cerebri which involves the right eye only. She subsequently lost vision in the left eye this weekend. She has light perception in the left eye, but could not see forms. She has numerous medication allergies."

Then came a laundry list of medical problems: "Systemic lupus erythematosus, cortical blindness, pseudotumor cerebri/status post lumboperitoneal shunt, right occipital neuralgia, oral moniliasis, hypokalemia, urinary tract infection."

On March 28, 1990, Lynn's report from the neurology clinic noted, "Our patient's headaches have gotten worse. Her left eye seems to be fading in and out more than before. She has dizziness, particularly when she stands up. She has no light perception of the right eye."

Many nights Lynn would cry herself to sleep. "Lord, please don't let me become totally blind," she prayed. "Please help me!"

Chapter 4

━━━━━ ✝ ━━━━━

Hand in Hand

Dick and Judy Gadd were on their second honeymoon. After years of taking their children on vacation to Myrtle Beach, South Carolina, they decided to sell their small business in Elkins, West Virginia, and move there permanently.

One night, walking hand in hand along the beach, Dick squeezed his wife's hand and said, "You know, life doesn't get much better than this."

Then in June 1991, something happened to shatter the dream. Dick noticed that he was passing blood. Immediately he went to a local doctor for an examination. "I was told there were suspicious growths in my bladder," says Gadd. "The doctor wanted me to see a urologist for a second opinion." The findings were confirmed.

In July 1991, biopsies showed numerous malignant growths. Some of them had already penetrated the muscles and wall of the bladder. Again, the physician recommended that Gadd get other opinions before discussing his options. Dick says, "I was told that my bladder must come out as well as the prostate. I hoped to avoid having an ostomy bag."

Dick and Judy, Methodist and Baptist by family background, summoned all the faith they could muster. Judy looked at the doctor and said, "He will be healed. Maybe not by your hands, but he will be healed."

The Prognosis

The couple drove back to West Virginia to visit with a urologist the family knew quite well. He agreed with the doctors' findings. At the advice of several doctors, Dick went to the Duke University Medical Center in Durham, North Carolina.

The doctors concluded that Dick's bladder, prostate, and appendix must be removed. "If all goes well," they told him, "we can reconstruct a new bladder from a portion of your intestines." This would mean that he could avoid having an ostomy bag.

In September 1991, Gadd returned to Duke for surgery. On the evening of the operation, an intravenous feeding tube was inserted into his wrist. "Somehow the IV damaged a nerve and infused into my arm," he says. "My entire left hand and arm were swollen. They looked as though they were going to explode."

Orthopedic surgeons worked on Dick's arm while he was in the operating room. For nine hours surgeons performed the removals and did reconstructive surgery. "They took two feet of my intestines and constructed a new bladder," Gadd says. "Then they installed a catheter."

The surgery was ruled a success. When the pathology reports came back, the doctors told Dick, "You're home free. There is no more cancer."

On the day Dick got the good news, his body suddenly told him something entirely different. "My temperature spiked to 105, and I began to experience extreme pain," says Dick. "The doctors rushed me to x ray thinking I might have pneumonia."

The test did not reveal the cause of the fever or the pain. "The high temperature continued, and I felt as if all the energy had been drained from my body," says Gadd.

Finally, the medical team diagnosed the problem as Candida, a yeast infection that developed from the surgery. It had affected his entire blood stream. "The physicians informed me that the infection was life-threatening since it could shut down a vital organ at any time," Gadd says. "They gave me a powerful medication that produced many side effects. I had severe chills, my body was shaking, and my fever continued."

To Dick, the new problems were much worse than the surgery. "I felt I was wasting away in a hospital bed and was begging the doctors to allow me to go home."

Finally, the physicians gave their approval for Gadd to return to Myrtle Beach. They arranged for home health care and a doctor to monitor his serious condition. Dick continued to take intravenous medication, but the suffering would not subside.

Why the Pain?

Even before he left the hospital for home, Dick began to feel severe pain in his back. The numerous scans, however, revealed nothing.

In October 1991, Gadd returned to Duke for removal of the catheter and to learn how to control his reconstructed bladder. But the doctors could find no cause for his continued back pain.

Adding to his growing list of problems, Dick's left hand had grown steadily worse. "I could not control it," Gadd says. "My fingers were numb, and my hand trembled uncontrollably. The fingers would not straighten out."

By this time Dick had lost fifty pounds. The high temperatures continued. Says Judy, "For several months he was either in bed, on the couch, or in a recliner."

In February 1992, when Dick returned to the hospital for a scheduled checkup, there was no improvement in his hand, and he continued to experience excruciating back pain. "It was almost impossible to use my hand. I was told that most likely it was permanently impaired," Gadd recalls.

During that visit, the medical specialists conducted one final test—a chest x ray. Then, two days later, Dick received a phone call. "Mr. Gadd, we need you to have an MRI as soon as possible."

When he questioned the urgency, Dick was told that he could be totally paralyzed at any moment. The specialists explained that his vertebrae were compressed, but they did not know the cause of this problem. "Be extremely cautious, and have the test immediately," they said.

After the MRI, a second identical test was ordered the next day. "Mr. Gadd, we want you to return to Duke as soon as possible for additional examinations and to see a cancer specialist," he was told.

Gadd returned to the medical center, and for two full days he had test after test. The diagnosis: a malignant mass in the back that had crushed the eighth and ninth thoracic vertebrae. He was told, "We need to start six weeks of radiation treatment immediately. We will follow that with chemotherapy."

Dick was told he could stay at a local motel and go to the hospital for his treatments. He told the doctors, "I can't do that. We have a teenage son at home, and I need to be with him."

There was another problem. The Gadds' insurance had expired, and they already owed nearly $50,000 in medical bills.

Dick and Judy returned to Myrtle Beach. "I was determined that any treatment I got I would get close to my home," Dick says. Judy told the doctors, "You don't understand how much faith we have. Dick is going to make it."

As she had done so many times, Judy reached out to hold Dick's hand. This time it was disfigured, but that didn't matter. "It's going to be all right," she whispered.

Chapter 5

✝

Marsha Needed a Miracle

Marsha Brantley, from Lawton, Oklahoma, had been sick for as long as she could remember.

"Since I was eighteen months old I have experienced severe pain in my legs, back, and joints. My mother recalls that I would constantly cry because the pain was so intense," she says. "I lacked the energy to participate in activities with other people. I simply learned to live with the chronic pain and fatigue."

The doctors were unable to diagnose Marsha's illness for thirty years.

Naming the Monster

In 1989 she went to the doctor with a skin rash, but tests revealed a far greater problem—lupus, a form of arthritis. Lupus directly affects a person's joints, causing swelling, severe pain, and stiffness. In Marsha's case, the disease affected the circulation in her fingers. They would turn blue and would feel cold.

The lupus also touched other parts of her body. Her eyes were extremely dry. So was her mouth. It reduced her energy level, leaving her weak and tired most of the time.

"I didn't even know what lupus was when they told me I had it," says Marsha.

Marsha's condition deteriorated rapidly. "I just couldn't function. I was trying to finish my degree but had to drop out of classes."

A Trio of Illnesses

As the medical testing continued, she was eventually diagnosed with Raynaud's disease, Sjögren's syndrome, and ankylosing spondylitis, which are all related to connective tissue disorders.

Raynaud's disease is a condition of the blood vessels in which exposure to cold causes the small arteries that supply the fingers and toes to contract suddenly. When this happens blood stops flowing to the digits, causing them to become pale. That is why Marsha's hands, feet, and nose would turn blue, cold, and numb. Then as the circulation was restored, these areas would be quite painful.

She also had Sjögren's syndrome, a malady that causes the moisture-producing glands of the body to atrophy, resulting in limited and sporadic production of saliva and tear secretion.

Ankylosing spondylitis causes bones and ligaments to fuse and become stiff. It can lead to a permanent curvature of the spine.

"My hips and shoulders were slowly fusing solid!" she says. "And lupus was causing severe pain and swelling of the rest of my body. Additionally, it had left me allergic to bright light, causing me to run high temperatures."

Bleak, Bleaker, Bleakest

Marsha reached the point where she could barely function. She had moved to Broken Arrow, Oklahoma, and her mother came to be with her.

"I had to spend from sixteen to eighteen hours a day in bed," she recalls. "I could not take care of myself. My hair was once very long, but it had to be cut when I could not even hold a hair dryer after washing it."

When she could no longer hold a purse, she began wearing a belt pack.

"I walked with a cane because my right knee and my right hip could hardly move. It was not long until I regressed so severely I had to use a wheelchair, if I got out of the house at all," she says. "My doctor said it would only be a matter of time before my hips fused completely, and I would have to use a wheelchair all of the time."

The doctor also felt that the lupus had involved the connective tissue in the brain, affecting her memory. "It was like I was being tortured daily, not knowing how severe the pain would be or what part of my body would not work."

The doctors had done all they could. Her family and friends had done all they could. Despite their love and compassion, Marsha felt helpless and alone.

"There was only one place left to turn," she says. "I placed my future in the hands of the Lord."

Marsha needed a miracle.

Chapter 6

———— ✝ ————

Charlie Had
Another Plan

Charlie McLain believed that when he won his battle with cancer, he would never again have to face such an enemy. But he didn't know what was waiting just ahead.

In 1984 the Tulsa, Oklahoma, mortgage and loan officer was diagnosed with Hodgkin's disease, a malignant disorder of the lymphoid tissue. He began a two-year ordeal with the cancer that included three surgeries and massive chemotherapy and radiation treatments.

"With the help of some marvelous physicians, the Lord brought me through," says Charlie.

His Hodgkin's disease was diagnosed as 4-A, which rarely goes into remission. When it did, he thought his health problems were over. After five years without a recurrence of cancer, Charlie was enjoying the best health of his life.

Then, in the first week of December 1990, McLain suddenly felt very ill. "I was unable to eat and had severe pain in my stomach," he says. The condition appeared without warning. He hoped the pain would subside, but it didn't. He knew something was wrong.

Two Unsuccessful Surgeries

On Wednesday evening, December 12, 1990, Mc-Lain went to the emergency room of Saint Francis Hospital in Tulsa and was admitted with abdominal distress.

The diagnosis was an intestinal blockage of the small bowel.

Three days later McLain had surgery, but the surgeons could find no blockage so they closed him up thinking everything would resolve itself. It didn't. "Nothing would pass through my system," he says, remembering it as if it were yesterday.

Following an exhaustive battery of tests, they finally found the blockage in an extremely unusual location. The emergency surgery which followed was assumed to be successful. The physicians discovered substantial aftereffects of the massive amounts of radiation from his earlier bout with cancer. These large doses had caused massive internal damage. His intestines were full of adhesions. As one of his doctors described it, "The radiation treatments from his lymphoma had left his intestinal walls scarred and thickened, causing them to stick to each other and twist and turn."

Charlie calls it being "fried."

That surgery, too, had been a failure. Charlie still

had a blockage. His fever climbed to 104, then 106. His lungs began filling with fluid and his kidneys began to shut down. His bowels no longer functioned.

"Christmas Eve is not the ideal time to have surgery," says Charlie, "but that is when they opened me up again."

The surgeons did not like what they saw. Said one of them, "The bowel was so thick and inflamed we just couldn't do the bypass, which was pretty rare. I was very concerned he might not make it." They knew Charlie was an extremely sick patient.

His team of medical experts included an oncologist, a gastroenterologist, two nephrologists, and surgeons.

Says Charlie's wife, Cyndii, "At that point we knew he was close to death."

First, they used a balloon catheter to enlarge the intestines to their normal size. Then they inserted a feeding tube and a waste drainage tube. The physicians hoped Charlie would become strong enough for another surgery. They knew they could not do it immediately, or he would not survive. Said an attending physician, "We hoped to do the next surgery in a couple of months if humanly possible."

"Get Me Home, and I'll Be Healed"

About forty-eight hours after the Christmas Eve surgery, the blockage remained unchanged. Charlie says, "I stayed in the hospital for about two more weeks while they tried to build my strength and increase my weight."

The doctors didn't express much optimism. One

of them told McLain, "Don't get in a hurry; you will be fighting this for a long, long time."

The surgeons told Charlie, "We've operated twice and the problem is still there. We can't do anything else, and frankly, even if you could get your body back in shape where we could operate again, we don't think you have enough intestines left that we can even bypass. We may have to remove your entire intestinal tract."

Charlie had another plan. "No," he told the doctors. "We don't need to do that. Get me home, and I'll be healed."

Since patients often make a quicker recovery in their own environment, the medical team decided to allow McLain to leave the hospital. It was the middle of January 1991 when Cyndii welcomed him back to their home in south Tulsa.

Instead of weighing his usual 228 pounds, Charlie now weighed only 170 pounds. "I was extremely weak," he recalls. "I couldn't raise my arm above my shoulder. It was almost impossible to comb my hair."

At home, Charlie was hooked to an IV for fifteen to eighteen hours a day. "I was thankful that during the last operation they had hooked up a feeding tube to my intestine and placed a gastric tube in my stomach. The blockage was between the two."

McLain doubts that the doctors paid much attention when he said, "Get me home, and I'll be healed." But Charlie believed that was about to happen.

Chapter 7

✝

No Relief in Sight

"They said the problem was in my head, but I knew it was in my arm," says Sarah Knapp, a licensed practical nurse from Johnston City, a small community in southern Illinois.

Every day, as part of her job, Sarah lifted heavy people and pulled heavy equipment. Then one day she told her husband, Donald, that she was beginning to feel unusual pains in her shoulder and arms. The pains got progressively worse.

"I remember the time I was helping lift a patient in bed when my hand started swelling," she says.

It took nearly nine months for doctors to determine what was wrong. She was diagnosed with thoracic outlet syndrome, a condition in which the nerves going out of the arm sockets are pinched by the bones and ribs. It causes severe pain and a "pins and needles" feeling in the fingers. One's grip becomes weak, and other hand movements are affected.

She was told that the major cause of the disease was the repetitive nature of her work.

"Surely, There Must Be an Answer"

"When you are hurting as much as I was, you will do almost anything to get rid of the pain," she says. "I had a football-shaped swelling on the back of my shoulder blade. One side of my chest was swollen nearly half again as big as my other side. I couldn't lie on my back, or on my right side."

Sarah was not able to hold a fork to eat. She was not able to shake hands.

At the Jewish Hospital in Louisville, Kentucky, Sarah had surgery for the problem. The surgeons removed her top rib, removed muscle from her neck, and performed a nerve release on her arm.

The surgery did not relieve her condition.

"The pain kept getting worse, and I continued to lose strength in my arm. The muscle in my right arm was deteriorating, and my hand began to curl up and lose its usefulness," she says. "The doctor told me I would probably never get better."

After Sarah returned home from the hospital, she felt more pain and increased numbness in her arm. "Day after day I would sit and hold my arm and cry."

Sarah wondered, "Will I have to spend the rest of my life in this condition? Surely, there must be an answer."

Chapter 8

✝

Is There Hope for Timothy?

Timothy Michael Mercer was not supposed to live.

He was born on July 11, 1990, four weeks premature at Florida Hospital. Doctors diagnosed his condition as "hypoplastic lungs with persistent pulmonary vascular hypertension."

Timothy's medical chart listed several additional problems: bilateral pneumothorax (a condition in which air leaks into a space between the lining of the lungs and the chest wall), bilateral hydronephrosis (the kidney becomes distended with urine due to a blockage or narrowing of the tubes that carry urine from the kidneys to the bladder), and distended urinary bladder.

Getting Off to a Bad Start

His grandmother, Ann Mercer, well remembers the day he was born. "His skin was blue when he was born. They rushed him out of delivery immediately after his birth. After examining Timothy, the doctor told his mother, Wanda, and me that there were so many things wrong with him that he wouldn't live through the night."

Little Timothy's lungs were not yet developed. When he was born, they were so small that the X ray would not pick them up. Because of an extremely high mortality rate in infants with hypoplastic lungs, not to mention all of his other complications, the doctors had virtually no hope for his recovery.

A Possible Solution

When a doctor from another hospital became aware of Timothy's condition, he suggested that Timothy be taken to Arnold Palmer Hospital and placed on a machine called ECMO (Extra Corporeal Membrane Oxygenation). It is essentially a heart and lung bypass machine, very similar to those used in heart bypass surgery.

The family members decided to move him, but his condition was not stable enough for the transfer. Doctors placed Timothy on a respirator in an attempt to expand his lungs. However, the respirator was set too high for his little body and his lungs suffered further damage.

Within a short time, however, the transfer was made. When Timothy arrived at Arnold Palmer Hospital, a baby had just been taken off the machine that Timothy needed making it possible for him to be evaluated.

The family listened as the doctor listed several criteria the baby must meet to be placed on the machine. The physician told them, "We will let you know in a couple of hours."

Timothy met only one of the criteria, but the doctors decided to try the machine anyway.

At 10:00 P.M. Ann Mercer was standing beside her grandson's bed. "Suddenly his heart stopped, and he quit breathing," she recalls. "I was hurried out of the room."

Immediately, they began CPR. They were able to resuscitate him. Timothy was stabilized and put on the machine. The doctor told the family that blood thinners were used on babies on ECMO, and if the brain, kidneys, or lungs started to bleed, he would have to suspend treatment. He also said that Timothy could only be on the machine for twenty-one days maximum.

When Timothy was on the ECMO unit, there were two large tubes that came out of his jugular vein. The blood was brought out of his body into an artificial kidney, up through an artificial heart, through an artificial lung, back down to a warming process, and back into his body. It did the work of his lungs.

Every day, it seemed a new and more challenging problem developed. On day five Timothy experienced a level one brain bleed. He survived that complication. However, the family was given no hope for Timothy's survival or well-being unless his lungs grew.

Which Way is Home?

The day finally arrived when Timothy was released from the hospital. He was on oxygen and a heart monitor constantly. Recalls Ann, "Someone had to be with him around the clock because we couldn't let him cry. If he cried, he would burn calories needed for his growth. Unless he gained weight, his lungs wouldn't grow."

After only eleven days he was rushed back to the hospital with respiratory failure. This happened again and again. Says Ann, "We had many midnight rides to the hospital, where he was turning blue and was not breathing."

It was almost as if the baby had two homes. After twenty-two days, he was discharged. Six days later he returned. This went on until the middle of October. When he was home he was attended by a nurse twice a day because of the severity of his condition.

At the end of October 1990, Timothy was in the hospital again. This time the doctors were going to return him to the respirator.

In November 1990, following release from the hospital, one of the doctors told his mother, "Take Timothy home and enjoy him as long as you can. If he goes into respiratory failure again, I doubt that his lungs are strong enough for him to pull through."

At that moment they had no idea what would happen to Timothy in the next few days. It would forever rewrite the medical history of his life.

Chapter 9

———— † ————

"I've Got to Talk to God"

"You've got to be kidding," said Doreen Maddeaux.

In November 1987, she went to the doctor because of an eye infection. As part of her exam he did a routine electrocardiogram (EKG) and what it revealed was startling. "I don't like what I see," said the doctor. "It looks as though you have had a silent heart attack."

Doreen, who lives in Willowdale, a suburb of Toronto, Ontario, couldn't believe the report. "It was a shock for me because I had rarely had a sick day in my entire life," she says.

A Family Trait

Her first thought was that she had been misdiagnosed. "I remembered that the machine had stopped once. They had to reload it and paste the pages back together," she recalls. Doreen had once been a medical lab technician and knew that mistakes could be made.

"Actually, I took the news very lightly," recalls Doreen. "I even had a stress test, and it did not show anything unusual."

After the original EKG, her doctor gave her a prescription that he wanted her to continue to take. She told him, "Why should I spend my money for medication when I'm not sick?"

Her physician, however, believed she should have additional tests. In December 1987, she had an angiogram, a procedure that enables blood vessels to be seen on film after the vessels have been filled with a substance that is opaque to X rays.

The angiogram showed that Doreen had coronary artery disease.

"Again, my reaction was one of unbelief, but it should not have been," says Doreen. "I came from a family with a history of heart disease on both sides. The average age of death was fifty-eight." She had just celebrated her fiftieth birthday.

Coronary artery disease afflicts the arteries that supply blood (and thus oxygen and food) to the heart muscle itself. The disease (atherosclerosis) causes the arteries to become laden with fatty deposits, harden, and become partially obstructed. This reduces the amount of blood that reaches the heart muscle and can lead to chest pain called angina pectoris, or worse, a heart attack that kills part of the heart muscle.

A Frightening Experience

Doreen and her doctors believed she could live with the disease. The physicians prescribed light medication and told Doreen to avoid excessive physical activity. The next month she took a trip to Israel without incident.

In October 1988, she traveled with a group to New York City. "On that trip my body began to tell me I had a serious problem," she remembers. "I was with people who were eighty years old, and I couldn't keep up with them."

Doreen was frightened that she was not going to make it back to Toronto. On the way home from the airport she went to a medical clinic for an exam.

Within a month she was rushed from her job to the emergency room of the hospital with unstable angina. Doreen spent the next fifty-two days in a coronary care unit and in intensive care. The next year she was under constant medical supervision. "I was told I would never be able to work again," she says.

"Lord! Help!"

The waiting list for bypass surgery was so long the doctors decided to do an angioplasty on two of her arteries. Angioplasty is a technique for treating the narrowing or blockage of an artery by introducing a balloon into the constricted area to widen it. Within three months her doctors had to perform the same procedure on other blocked arteries.

Her condition became serious enough that in October 1989, Doreen had a single bypass operation, because the other arteries were too small to be bypassed. The doctors went into her leg to find a small artery to bypass the others, but could not find a suitable one.

Coronary artery bypass graft surgery is an operation in which a section of vein is removed and sewn onto the aorta, the large artery leaving the heart. The other end of the vein is then attached to a branch of the coronary artery. In effect, this procedure detours the blood around the damaged or blocked areas of the coronary arteries to increase the blood flow to the heart.

"The surgery was the scariest thing I had ever experienced," says Doreen. "I woke up to a machine pumping my heart, and I was hardly able to speak or think. I tried to pray but could not seem to say more than one word at a time. I said, 'Lord! Help!'"

A Deteriorating Situation

The next year Doreen was rushed to the hospital with severe breathing difficulties. "I was always short of breath and found it getting more and more difficult to shop for just one small bag of groceries," she said.

When the cardiograms showed a lack of oxygen in the bypassed areas her doctors ordered a Thallium Stress Test. In this procedure, radioactive metallic elements reveal areas of heart muscle that have poor blood supply or that have been damaged.

Her condition seemed to stabilize, but in May 1992, Doreen had to call 911 and was again rushed by ambulance to the hospital. Tests showed that her heart condition had deteriorated.

The doctor's report states: "Mrs. Maddeaux has

serious coronary artery disease. Unfortunately she
has not done particularly well with bypass surgery
and with angioplasty. Certainly her problem at this
moment could not be solved by angioplasty, and
she would require bypass."

He also wrote, "She had a very bad stress test
suggesting a limited exercise tolerance and of
course this is happening in her day to day life."

She had only one narrow artery being supplied by
small collateral arteries feeding the heart. Another
cardiac surgery seemed to be the only hope, but the
doctor left that decision to her.

Doreen dreaded the thought of another operation, but she didn't know what else to do. "I was
turned down by two excellent surgeons," she says,
"because they didn't want to take the risk." She
finally saw a surgeon who believed the surgery
could be accomplished, but he told her, "We cannot guarantee how long it will stay effective."

In July 1992, she was again taken to the emergency
room because of a lack of oxygen. "I lost my ability
to speak," says Doreen.

Her cardiogram showed trouble. She was put on
morphine and nitro drip and sent to the coronary
care unit. "The doctor begged me to consent to the
operation right away, but I said, 'No.'"

"You Have to Give Me Three Weeks"

Doreen, who had been a Christian since 1961,
began to exercise her faith. "I knew that God was
going to heal me," she said.

After several days in the heart ward she knew the
physicians would not let her out of the hospital until

she consented to the operation. "I knew it was a life and death situation," she recalls.

Her sister, Pat, came to the coronary care unit and told her, "Doreen, it's too late. You have no other choice."

She told Pat, "If the operation is not going to last more than three months to a year, why do it?" Then she added, "I'd rather just go to be with the Lord."

At one point there was a "red alert" when medical personnel came from all parts of the hospital. "They began to hook me up to special equipment, and I became frightened."

Doreen remembers looking up and asking, "Am I going now, Lord?" She prayed, "God, either take me or heal me." She was prepared to die if that was what the Lord wanted. "But somehow God gave me the courage to fight back," she says.

She told the doctor, "I didn't say I'm not going to have the operation, but you have to give me three weeks."

The physician looked puzzled. "What do you want three weeks for?" he asked.

"Because I've got to talk to God," she told him. "I can't die before I talk to God."

He said, "Talk to God here."

She responded, "I can't. I've got to get out."

Doreen Maddeaux couldn't possibly tell him what she was about to do.

Chapter 10

✝

Too Frightened to Speak

"It's all right," the teacher said. "Just take your time."

The little boy standing in front of the class was having a horrible time reading a story to his classmates.

"The h-h-house was p-p-painted white," he read from his schoolbook.

He suffered from a stuttering problem that would flare up when there was the slightest amount of tension or pressure. And standing before his classmates was humiliating.

After school, the children would mock and taunt him until he wanted to run and hide.

That boy was me.

A Painful Experience

I was born and raised in the historic Mediterranean city of Jaffa, Israel. My parents were of Greek and Armenian ancestry, and I was taught by monks and nuns in Catholic schools.

At the age of five or six it was apparent to me, and to those around me, that I had a serious problem. When I was calm, or with a friend I knew very well, I could speak for a period of several minutes without stammering. Then, when fear or tension came, the condition would be triggered again.

The stuttering was especially pronounced when I was in the presence of an authority figure or in a public place. Usually, I would stutter over one or two words. But there were times when it seemed to take me forever to say a complete sentence.

As a young boy, when people would come to see my father, I would hide under a table or under the bed so people would not make fun of me. I couldn't bear the thought of having them laugh at me because of my impediment.

In school, as the years went by, I rarely ever volunteered to answer a question. When I was required to make an oral presentation, it was a painful experience. It was especially difficult during exam times.

I remember how the teachers would threaten the students with punishment if they laughed at me when I spoke. I got through it, and so did my classmates. But after class one or two of them would pass by and mock me, pretending to stutter.

The children didn't know how deeply they were hurting me. I'm sure they did not mean any harm. At times I felt so angry I wished I could retaliate.

My teachers, especially the nuns, were supportive

and understanding. One day some of the sisters placed their fingers on my ears, thinking that if I didn't hear any external noise I might be able to speak without stuttering. If it helped at all, it didn't last long.

The most devastating aspect of stuttering was what it did to my self-image. To me, it was as crippling as a physical problem. I could almost feel my personality being destroyed.

"Yes, Sir!"

As a child, or even as a teenager, there was never a time when I could sit down and have a conversation with my father. People who have been raised in a Middle Eastern family will understand what I am saying. He was the ultimate authority figure in my life.

Father would say "Do this!" or "Don't do that!"

I would only say, "Yes, sir!" or "No, sir!"

When I needed to approach my father about something, I became frozen with fear. He would usually say something like, "Speak it out, son."

He was not the type of person who would ask, "What happened in school today?" or "Tell me what you have been doing."

Wham! It Hit Me

In 1968, one year after Israel's Six Day War, our family emigrated to Toronto, Canada. As a teenager at Georges Vanier Secondary School, my stuttering continued.

Then in February 1972 my life was transformed by an encounter with Christ at a morning prayer meeting conducted by students at the school. Later that day I opened the pages of a big black Bible that had not been used in our home for years. After reading the Gospels nonstop for several hours I found myself saying out loud, "Jesus, come into my heart. Please, Lord Jesus, come into my heart."

I thank God He did.

Later that week I went with my newfound Christian friends to their church. It wasn't a typical church. The people who attended were an exuberant throng of Christians who met every Thursday in St. Paul's Cathedral, an Anglican church in downtown Toronto.

As a teenager, I found clever ways to disguise the fact that I stuttered. Sometimes I tried to use mind over matter. I had discovered that if I didn't dwell on my problem I could speak quite a while without stuttering. But when the stammering hit me, it was out of my control.

I did everything possible to avoid conversing with people who might cause this nervous reaction. Public speaking, of course, was out of the question.

As a new Christian I became totally involved in the services. I even joined the large singing group on the platform. When you sing, you don't stutter.

One night, the pastor's wife, asked me to take part in the service. "Benny," she said, "I'd like you to read the twenty-first chapter of Revelation."

She had no idea that I had a severe stuttering problem.

There were more than two thousand people in the service that night. I wanted to say "No," but didn't want to disappoint her. My eyes closed and

I thought, "Oh, dear God, I am going to get up there and make a fool out of myself."

That evening I walked to the microphone and began to read aloud. After about two or three lines, "Wham!" It hit me. Tears began to fill my eyes, and I was paralyzed with panic. Everything seemed to fall apart.

Fortunately for me this was a very sensitive woman and she recognized my plight. She quickly began leading the audience in singing rather than let me stand there any longer. I walked back to my seat totally humiliated.

They didn't ask me to read Scripture again.

During those days I attended a Bible study that met every Saturday morning. There were about twenty of us who attended. As part of the teaching, the group leader would start on one side of the room and ask each student to read a verse or two of Scripture. Then he would comment on it, and move to the next person in the circle.

Just about the time it was my turn to read, I would quietly get up and go to the restroom. Week after week, for nearly a year I used the same routine. I would wait outside the door of the classroom until I knew my turn had passed. Then I'd return to the group.

Finally, the teacher took me aside and talked with me. I could tell he was a little upset. He said, "Look Benny, this is a class. You're always going to the bathroom at the same time." He said, "Nobody cares about your stuttering."

He knew what I was doing. They all knew.

"But Lord, I Can't Talk!"

Just before Christmas 1973, I traveled to Pittsburgh, Pennsylvania, to attend a meeting of evangelist Kathryn Kuhlman. When I returned home that night, in my bedroom, I had a personal encounter with the Holy Spirit unlike anything I had ever experienced. If you have read *Good Morning, Holy Spirit*, you understand the depth of what happened.

Someone recently asked, "Benny, did you notice any difference in your stuttering problem after the Spirit came into your life?"

In April 1974 after four glorious months of my continuing encounter with the Spirit, the Lord spoke to me in an audible voice. He said, "Preach the gospel."

My response, of course, was, "But Lord, I can't talk."

In the months that followed, the Lord continued to speak to me through the Word, through visions, and through the Holy Spirit. Finally in November 1974, I could no longer avoid the subject. I said to the Lord, "I will preach the gospel on one condition: that You will be with me in every service." And then I reminded Him, "Lord, You know that I can't talk." I worried constantly about my speech problem and the fact that I was going to be an embarrassment.

Then one afternoon, the first week of December, I was visiting the home of some friends.

It was the first time I felt led to tell anyone the full story about my encounters with the Holy Spirit. Since these people were my friends, and I was totally relaxed, there was little trace of my stuttering. Even before I had finished, one of them said,

"Benny, tonight you must come to our church and share this." They had a fellowship of about a hundred people who met in a local church.

That night I was introduced to the group, and for the first time in my life I stood behind a pulpit to preach.

The instant I opened my mouth, I felt something touch my tongue and loosen it. I began to proclaim God's Word with absolute fluency.

Two of my friends who knew of my stuttering problems were at the service. After church they both said to me, "We couldn't believe how well you talked. You didn't even stutter once."

I knew what they meant.

Later that night in my room I thought, "The stuttering must have left because the presence of the Lord was on me tonight. Surely it will come back." But it didn't. From that moment the stuttering was gone. All of it.

"I'm Going to Die"

My parents, especially my father, had no idea that I was healed because there was virtually no communication between us in the home. They had practically disowned me when I gave my heart to the Lord almost three years earlier.

Even my brothers and sisters were forbidden to talk to me. My mother was the only person I had limited conversation with, but I rarely stuttered in her presence anyway.

From the moment I first began to preach I started to receive invitations to minister. Week after week I was speaking at churches and special meetings. If my parents had known what was happening, I'm sure they would have thrown me out on the street.

Several months later, in April 1975, my mother and father somehow saw an advertisement in the *Toronto Star* that I was preaching in a Pentecostal church on the west side of town.

I was sitting on the platform that Sunday night when suddenly I looked up during the song service. I could hardly believe my eyes. There were my mother and father being ushered to a seat. I thought, "This is it. I'm going to die."

That night I preached under the power of God's anointing, but I couldn't bring myself to look in the direction of my mom and dad. Just before the end of the service they stood up and walked out the back door.

I drove around the city until two in the morning, hoping my parents would be in bed when I got home. As I quietly unlocked and opened the front door, I was startled to see my mother and father seated on the couch in front of me.

I was stricken with fear and looked for a place to sit down. My father was the first to speak. "Son," he said, "how can we become like you?"

My mother began to cry. And for the next two hours I shared the plan of salvation with them and was able to lead my parents to Christ.

My daddy said, "Benny, do you know what convinced me?" He told me that when I began preaching, he turned to my mother and said, "That's not your son. Your son can't talk! His God must be real." He didn't know that I had been totally healed of stuttering.

The Scars Were Gone

Several months after my parents were saved, the Lord began dealing with me in a special way. He said, "Benny, I want you to forgive your father for everything he has done to you."

As a child I was so destroyed by my stuttering that it was almost impossible to face the world—or myself. I could still remember my father saying, "Of all my children, you are the one who will never make it." His words only added to my problem.

That night, the Lord spoke to me about "forgetting it all." It was painful because suddenly all the memories flashed back, and I said, "Lord, I can't."

The anger that surfaced inside me was far greater than I imagined. "Lord, I love him," I cried, "but I am still so hurt by all the things he did and said."

The Lord told me, "You make the decision, and I'll do the rest."

I said, "I don't feel forgiveness in my heart, but I'll trust You to release me from all my past anger and hurt."

That night I made a decision to forgive my father. The moment I did, I felt as though a hand reached into my being and pulled things out of me that I cannot describe or explain.

From that moment I felt a total release. I was at peace with my father, and the scars that had crippled me were totally erased.

My healing was complete.

Part Two

The Bible's Teaching About Miracles

Chapter 11

———— ✝ ————

The Start of Your Miracle

From the moment I was healed of stuttering, God gave me an unquenchable appetite for the Word. I had a hunger to know everything possible about the Lord's miracle power.

Day after day, night after night, I devoured Scripture. The more I read, the more I realized that God did not intend for His children to live with infirmities. He wanted them restored, made whole.

The day came that I prayed, "Lord, just as You healed me, I give You my life so that others may know Your salvation, Your Spirit, Your anointing, and Your miracle-working power."

Did I have questions? Yes. There was much I needed the Lord to reveal through His Word.

- How did disease first enter the world?
- What is the relationship between sin and sickness?

- Is it God's will for us to be healed?
- What happened on the cross for healing?
- What is the role of the blood of Christ in healing?
- Why did Christ's body need to be broken?
- Can a person lose his miracle?
- Is forgiveness required for healing?
- What is the relationship between our soul and our health?
- Does the Lord have any conditions for a miracle?
- What is the connection between healing and worship?
- What is the role of faith?
- What does the Word say about keeping our healing?

The story of creation leaves no doubt that God formed a beautiful world that was free of sickness and disease—even death. "Then God saw everything that He had made, and indeed it was very good" (Gen. 1:31).

How did sin enter the world? Scripture makes it clear that when God created Adam he was not a sick man, but was full of health and life. But because Adam sinned every man and woman is a partaker in that original sin. Adam's actions brought both sickness and death to the human family. "Therefore, just as through one man sin entered the world, and death through sin, and thus death spread to all men, because all sinned" (Rom. 5:12).

Sin brought sickness and death. And since that moment of Adam's transgression there has been a penalty associated with man's failure to obey God. Israel, for example, suffered sickness because of their sins. God said through the prophet Micah,

"Therefore I will also make you sick by striking you, by making you desolate because of your sins" (Mic. 6:13).

More Than a Ransom

God's plan to redeem man was to send His Son to be born as a man and to die on the cross for our salvation. But what happened at Calvary was even *more*. As we will discover, Christ not only brought redemption but provided for our healing.

You may ask, "Since sickness came to the earth through Adam, doesn't that mean that every person must experience illness?"

Not at all. Sickness may be all around us, but it is not God's will for His people to live in sickness. The Cross made provision for both our salvation and our healing. Jesus shed His blood for our sin, but His body was broken for our sicknesses.

The prophecies of the Old Testament foretold what Christ would endure for our healing. "Who has believed our report? / And to whom has the arm of the Lord been revealed? / For He shall grow up before Him as a tender plant, / And as a root out of dry ground. / He has no form or comeliness; / And when we see Him, / There is no beauty that we should desire Him" (Isa. 53:1–2).

Jesus, the "arm of the Lord," was to come out of a spiritually dead Israel—as a "root out of dry ground."

Before the crucifixion the Lord was whipped and beaten. As was prophesied in Isaiah 50:6, His beard was torn from His face. His form was so disfigured and His face so distorted the people could not recognize Him. Psalm 129:3 goes on to say, "The plowers plowed on my back; / They made their furrows long." So we can see from this description how badly our Lord was beaten. That is why Mary Magdalene did not know Him in the Garden. The last time she saw Him He had been beaten so badly she could not believe it was the same person.

The prophet wrote: "He is despised and rejected by men, / A man of sorrows and acquainted with grief. / And we hid, as it were, our faces from Him; / He was despised, and we did not esteem Him. / Surely He has borne our griefs / And carried our sorrows; / Yet we esteemed Him stricken, / Smitten by God, and afflicted" (Isa. 53:3–4).

Then we learn why this must take place. "But He was wounded for our transgressions, / He was bruised for our iniquities; / The chastisement for our peace was upon Him, / And by His stripes we are healed" (Isa. 53:5).

Many people fail to comprehend what really happened at Calvary. When we talk about salvation, we cannot ignore that God also provided for our healing.

The great ransom that was both prophesied and fulfilled was for more than spiritual salvation. Scripture tells us in Job 33:24; "Then He is gracious unto him, and saith, / 'Deliver him from going down to the pit; / I have found a ransom'" (KJV). So, God sent His Son to be a ransom and to deliver us from the pit of sin. But there's more! Look at Job 33:25 where we are also promised healing through the same ransom. "His flesh shall be fresher than a child's: / He shall return to the days of his youth" (KJV).

I believe God's plan includes salvation as well as provision for our healing.

Believing and Behaving

The New Testament is filled with accounts of miracles that accompanied the ministry of Christ and His followers. When healing came, however, it was almost always tied to both salvation and living a righteous life.

When Jesus healed the man at the pool of Bethesda who had an infirmity for thirty-eight years, "Afterward Jesus found him in the temple, and said to him, 'See, you have been made well. Sin no more, lest a worse thing come upon you'" (John 5:14).

You may say, "Please Lord, I desperately need a miracle!" But are you prepared to live according to His Word? When Christ heals you, He asks that you walk uprightly.

Should we expect to remain healed if we continue in our sin?

I recall the story of a woman in Los Angeles who was healed of deafness. God opened her ears in a healing service conducted by Aimee Semple Mc-Pherson during the earlier part of this century.

Several weeks later the deafness returned and the woman came back to one of the evangelist's meetings. Through a friend she asked, "Why is it that I only heard for a few weeks?"

Aimee asked the person who was with her, "Well, what did she do after she was healed?"

"Oh, she went back to work," the friend answered.

"Where does she work?" the evangelist wanted to know.

"She is a barmaid in a local tavern," was the reply.

Said Aimee, "Do you think God opened her ears to go back and listen to filth again?"

We should never forget that after Christ met the woman caught in adultery, He told her, "Go and sin no more" (John 8:11).

Who Is to Blame?

When we say that sickness came into the world because of Adam's fall, we should also realize that not all illness is the result of sin.

I have met many people who became sick because of their foolishness—and blatant disregard for the basic laws of health. They were ill, not because they had sinned, but because they did not treat their bodies properly. This is true of Christians and sinners alike.

Your physician, for example, may tell you to avoid fatty foods because your arteries are being clogged. If you fail to heed the warning, don't blame Satan for causing a heart attack. By the same measure, a person who knows that smoking causes lung cancer should not be smoking three packs a day.

It has always seemed rather presumptuous to me that people expect God to heal them when their own disobedience was the cause of their problem.

Prerequisites to Healing

I am always thrilled to read faith-building Scriptures that talk about our healing.

But many people fail to recognize that there are *prerequisites* to healing. In other words, the Lord will do His part when we do ours.

How can we become ready to receive a miracle? Here's what the Word says. "Bless the LORD, O my soul; / And all that is within me, bless His holy name!

/ Bless the LORD, O my soul, / And forget not all His benefits: / Who forgives all your iniquities, / Who heals all your diseases. . ." (Ps. 103:1-3).

The LORD promises us even more. He is the God "Who redeems your life from destruction, / Who crowns you with loving kindness and tender mercies, / Who satisfies your mouth with good things, / So that your youth is renewed like the eagle's. / The LORD executes righteousness / And justice for all who are oppressed" (Ps. 103:4-6).

When does your miracle start? When you begin to *"bless the Lord"* from the depths of your soul—from all that is within you.

It is understandable that when we are in the midst of a personal crisis, we can only think about crying out for help. Some people call on the Lord as if they were dialing "911" in an emergency. They approach the Lord by focusing on their problem. "Oh Lord," they say, "I know I am not worthy, but I desperately need you now."

Instead, we need to spend time praising and worshiping God for who He is. We should be saying, "Thank You Lord for shedding Your blood on the cross. Thank You Lord for redeeming my life from destruction. I praise You for Your healing power."

After blessing Him, Scripture tells us to *"forget not all His benefits"* (v. 2).

Look, there are seven benefits we are to remember! We serve a God who:

1. Forgives our iniquities (v. 3)
2. Heals our diseases (v. 3)
3. Redeems our life from destruction (v. 4)

4. Crowns our life with loving kindness and tender mercies (v. 4)
5. Satisfies our mouth with good things (v. 5)
6. Renews our youth like the eagle's (v. 5)
7. Defends us (v. 6)

As the Word makes so obvious, the benefits not only deal with our salvation, but with our health. And we are told to remember *all* of them.

When people forget what God has done, they limit His blessing. The children of Israel learned that lesson. "Yes, again and again they tempted God, / And limited the Holy One of Israel. / They did not remember His power: / The day when He redeemed them from the enemy" (Ps. 78:41-42).

Don't let another moment pass without pausing to bless the Lord and to remember His benefits.

The Keys to Your Miracle

In addition to praising a merciful God and recognizing what He has given us, there are some specific things we can do that will prepare us for God's healing touch.

First: Turn away from those who reject God's power.

How can we expect to be healed if we surround ourselves with people of unbelief? If you read God's Word, there should be no question of the action you must take. Scripture tells us that in the last days there would be people "having a form of godliness but denying its power. And from such people turn away!" (2 Tim. 3:5).

When you live in an atmosphere of unbelief it

does not take much to devastate you. The Bible says "Wisdom is better than weapons of war; / But one sinner destroys much good" (Eccl. 9:18). How many sinners does it take to cause destruction? *One.* Turn away from such people.

When you realize the power of both the spoken and the written word, you'll avoid those who would destroy your faith. Where should you turn? "So then faith comes by hearing, and hearing by the word of God" (Rom. 10:17).

Second: When you seek for a miracle, ask in faith.

We need to remove the "if" from our prayer. The Word says: "But let him ask in faith, with no doubting, for he who doubts is like a wave of the sea driven and tossed by the wind. For let not that man suppose that he will receive anything from the Lord" (James 1:6-7).

If you waiver, don't expect to receive much from the Lord. Instead, ask in faith knowing it is His perfect will to heal you.

Third: Turn your faith loose.

Many times when I'm ministering I can actually *see* people's faith. I can see it in their eyes—they are about to take some action to release their faith.

One night at a crusade I was in the middle of the message when suddenly my attention was drawn to a young man seated in the front row. He had a brace on his leg and a crutch leaning on his chair. But I could see a man whose faith was so alive that his countenance seemed to be bubbling.

I stopped my message and said, "Sir, I want you to stand up in the name of the Lord Jesus."

Not only did he stand, he tore off the brace and began to run around the front of the auditorium. The moment he heard the words "stand up," he turned his faith loose.

That's exactly how it happened in New Testament times. Once when the apostle Paul was preaching in Lystra, there was a man present who was "a cripple from his mother's womb, who had never walked" (Acts 14:8).

Scripture records that "This man heard Paul speaking. Paul, observing him intently and seeing that he had faith to be healed, said with a loud voice, 'Stand up straight on your feet!' And he leaped and walked" (vv. 9–10).

Do you recall the story of the ten lepers who met Jesus as He was traveling through their small village? Standing at a distance, they "lifted up their voices and said, 'Jesus, Master, have mercy on us!'" (Luke 17:13).

When the Lord Jesus saw them, He said, "'Go, show yourselves to the priests.' And so it was that as they went, they were cleansed" (v. 14).

When were they cleansed? As they *went*. They turned their faith loose.

If I were to ask you to tell me your greatest need, what would it be? Whatever the problem, it is vital that you come to the Lord with praise, with thanksgiving, and with faith that is alive.

It's the start of your miracle.

Chapter 12

✝

It's God's Will

As a minister of the gospel who takes God at His Word, I have spoken words of faith and healing hundreds of times. From Sweden to Singapore, from Bogota to Baltimore, I have seen people in pain and despair receive miracles from the Lord. Instantly, they were healed as they believed.

I believe it is not only God's will for you to be healed, but it is His will that you live in health until He calls you home (see Job 5:26).

If you are looking for a book to help you rationalize and justify your infirmities, this volume is not for you. I am not one who prays, "If it be your will, Lord, grant healing to this person."

It *is* His will! You will never hear me pray such faith-destroying words as "If it be Your will, Lord, heal them." God intends for you to rise and be healed. Today. Tomorrow. Always!

What the Lord desires for you has not changed from the time He held the greatest "miracle service" recorded in the Old Covenant. When God called His people, Israel, out of Egypt, they were sick and afflicted with infirmities. They were slaves who were undernourished and had been cruelly treated. But when God visited His people, something marvelous happened.

He brought them out of bondage and instantly, "there was not one feeble person among their tribes" (Ps. 105:37 KJV). I believe this verse clearly states that God's people were healed by one touch of His mighty hand at that moment.

God has not changed. Millions today are leaving their bondage and sin to find new life with Christ. God wants His children not only to come out of darkness, but also to come out of *sickness*.

When God delivered the children of Israel from Egypt, they were a healed people. And something more. The first covenant God made with them was a covenant of healing. After the total healing of the multitude, the first message they heard from God as they crossed the Red Sea was: "I am the LORD who heals you" (Ex. 15:26).

"Look at the Tree"

The lesson God demonstrated to the children of Israel concerning healing is profound. The Israelites had gone three days without finding water. And "when they came to Marah, they could not drink the waters of Marah, for they were bitter. Therefore the name of it was called Marah (or bitter). And the people complained against Moses, saying, 'What shall we drink?' So he cried out to the LORD, and the LORD showed him a tree; and when he cast it into the waters, the waters were made sweet. There He made a statute and an ordinance for them. And there He tested them, and said, 'If you diligently heed the voice of the LORD your God and do what is right in His sight, give ear to His commandments and keep all His statutes, I will put none of the diseases on you which I have brought on the Egyptians. For I am the LORD who heals you'" (Ex. 15:23–26).

They came out of Egypt healed! But they began murmuring and complaining about their circumstances. God gave them a warning and said that murmuring would produce sickness. What He meant was "if you will not murmur, I will not permit sickness to come on you," which means *they were already healed*.

The symbols found in this story carry an exciting message. When Moses cried out to the Lord, God showed him a tree. I believe it was because the tree represents the cross. God commanded him to cast the tree into the waters and immediately the water became sweet, no longer bitter. In Scripture, water sometimes represents people. "Sweetness" speaks of healing and health.

It was as if God was saying, "Take the cross (tree), cast it upon the people (waters), and they will be healed (made sweet)." Today, without the cross, there can be no healing. Before God Almighty healed the waters, He showed them the tree. Before we can receive our healing, we must look at the cross.

Did sickness ever return to the Israelites? Yes. But it was not God who sent it. Sickness was caused by their sin. In Numbers 21, the Bible says that when they turned their backs on righteousness, they were bitten by serpents.

The story of the Cross contains great symbolism. I believe God sent His Son to Calvary for both the healing of your soul and the healing of your body. As the crown of thorns was placed on His head, He bled for the healing of your mind and for your thought life. As He was whipped, His back was torn for your diseases.

If He bore, or carried away, our sickness, why should we attempt to carry what has already been placed on Him? It is gone. He has taken it away.

Often, in Scripture, when salvation came to a man or woman it was accompanied by healing.

Do you remember the Lord Jesus saying to Nicodemus, "And as Moses lifted up the serpent in the wilderness, even so must the Son of Man be lifted up" (John 3:14)? He was referring to an important story in the Old Testament that establishes this principle: *When sin enters, with it comes sickness.* And something more: *When sin departs, it takes sickness with it.*

"Look at the Cross"

"And the people spoke against God and against Moses: 'Why have you brought us up out of Egypt to die in the wilderness? For there is no food and no water, and our soul loathes this worthless bread.' So the LORD sent fiery serpents among the people, and they bit the people; and many of the people of Israel died. Therefore the people came to Moses, and said, 'We have sinned, for we have spoken against the LORD and against you; pray to the LORD that He take away the serpents from us.' So Moses prayed for the people. Then the LORD said to Moses, 'Make a fiery serpent, and set it on a pole; and it shall be that everyone who is bitten, when he looks at it, shall live'" (Num. 21:5–8). When you and I disobey the Lord, we can expect the serpents to bite (Eccl. 10:8). What God was saying, centuries before Calvary, was that even if you are bitten by the serpent, all you need to do is look again to the cross.

First, in Exodus 15:23, God showed him a tree. The second time in Numbers 21:8 the Lord told Moses to make a fiery serpent and set it upon a pole. "Then the LORD said to Moses, 'Make a fiery serpent, and set it on a pole; and it shall be that everyone who is bitten, when he looks at it, shall live.'" Each time, healing came by looking at the cross. Do you want to be healed? Do you want to know God's divine power that can give you life and health? Turn to Calvary.

The longer I study God's Word, the more convinced I am that a Christian should not be sick. If it is the will of God for me to be sick then Jesus took my sicknesses in vain.

Is it the Lord's will for me to live in sin? Of course not. For me to say, "It is God's will for me to be sick," would be like saying, "It is God's will for me to live in sin." But that's not His plan. I believe His perfect will for me is health and healing for the rest of my days just as I am confident He wants me to walk righteously. Now, do I always walk righteously? No, I make mistakes, repent and He forgives me. Do I enjoy complete and perfect health? No, I get sick, go to the Lord asking for His healing touch and He heals me.

Forgiven and Healed

When God forgives He also includes the provision for healing. The psalmist wrote: "Bless the LORD, O my soul, / And forget not all His benefits: / Who forgives all your iniquities, / Who heals all your diseases" (Ps. 103:2–3). With one touch, God forgives and heals.

When Jesus looked at the man who was crippled, He said, "'Which is easier, to say to the paralytic, "Your sins are forgiven you," or to say, "Arise, take up your bed and walk"? But that you may know that the Son of Man has power on earth to forgive sins'; He said to the paralytic, 'I say to you, arise, take up your bed, and go your way to your house.' And immediately he arose, took up the bed, and went out in the presence of them all, so that all were amazed and glorified God, saying, 'We never saw anything like this!'" (Mark 2:9–12).

Again, when the Lord forgives sin, He always includes healing. That is why James said, "Is anyone among you sick? Let him call for the elders of the church, and let them pray over him, anointing him with oil in the name of the Lord. And the prayer of faith will save the sick, and the Lord will raise him up. And if he has committed sins, he will be forgiven" (James 5:14–15).

It is simultaneous. Just one touch, one breath, from the Lord is all you need. *God saves and He heals. God forgives and He heals.*

We need to personalize the words of the psalmist

and repeat them again and again: "He forgives all my iniquities; He heals all my diseases."

He promised that "the inhabitant will not say, 'I am sick'; / the people who dwell in it will be forgiven their iniquity" (Isa. 33:24). And He does not intend for the problem to return. God has also promised that He will actually remove sickness from our presence. "So you shall serve the LORD your God, and He will bless your bread and your water. And I will take sickness away from the midst of you" (Ex. 23:25).

"My son, give attention to my words. . . . For they are life to those who find them, / And health to all their flesh" (Prov. 4:20,22).

Scripture clearly teaches that your body belongs to God, and it was designed to glorify Him. "For you were bought at a price; therefore glorify God in your body and in your spirit, which are God's" (1 Cor. 6:20). He wants to make you whole in every way.

Let me ask again: Is it the will of God that you walk in health? That's what the man with leprosy wanted to know. "And there came a leper to him, beseeching him, and kneeling down to him, and saying unto him, 'If thou wilt, thou canst make me clean.' And Jesus, moved with compassion, put forth his hand, and touched him, and saith unto him, 'I will; be thou clean'" (Mark 1:40–41 KJV), and He is still saying, "I will."

Chapter 13

————— † —————

Your Wall of Protection

Wouldn't it be wonderful if we could build a barricade that would shield us from sickness and disease? What you are about to discover is that a wall of protection has already been constructed. The provision has already been made.

As a young man in Toronto, I knew I had been converted and called to the ministry. But I had no knowledge of what I am teaching you now. Actually, I did not believe it. I thought that to be sick was to be saintly, that if you lie in a bed of affliction, God will use you for His glory.

I soon discovered, however, that our bodies were created to exalt and honor God Almighty. "For you were bought at a price; therefore glorify God in your body and in your spirit, which are God's" (1 Cor. 6:20). This discovery leads me to believe that if the

Lord Jesus was bruised and broken for my healing, then why should I carry that burden?

The Power of Believing

I firmly believe the Lord wants us to live in total health. It is time to believe, proclaim, and start living where you can say, "Sickness is not mine and I will not tolerate it under any circumstances!" When that message begins to stir within your soul, sickness will have to flee.

Four Simple Laws

God does not want you to be sick. In fact, in Exodus 15 He makes a covenant with you and tells you that if you keep that covenant you'll be healed. He will build a wall of protection around you.

To be specific, the Lord has established four simple laws—just four. If you obey them, you will live in health. And when sickness comes, you'll command it to leave your body.

God's four laws of healing are found in one powerful verse of Scripture. He says, "If you diligently heed the voice of the LORD your God and do what is right in His sight, give ear to His commandments and keep all His statutes, I will put none of the diseases on you which I have brought on the Egyptians. For I am the LORD who heals you" (Ex. 15:26).

For the first time in Scripture, God here introduces Himself as our healer, and He presents us with the four conditions we must meet to be healed. Condition Number One: *Heed.* You must "hearken" to the voice of the Lord. In Hebrew, the word means both to "hear and declare." You must hear it, speak it, and confess it. The importance of this first step cannot be overlooked.

Condition Number Two: *Do*. The Lord demands that you do what is right in His sight. The word *do* in Hebrew means "to make, to become, and to have charge of." So, dear friends, the Lord demands action on our part. And healing begins to happen as we obey the Word.

Condition Number Three: *Give ear*. The meaning in the original language is "ponder." God requires commitment on your part to meditate upon His commandments.

Condition Number Four: *Keep*. The Hebrew says "to guard, protect, and preserve" His Word. This is a prerequisite to healing.

What does God promise as a result of meeting these conditions? He says that He will heal you. If you hear the Word, confess it, commit fully to His laws, protect the Word, and make it your own, God says you will live in complete health.

God has offered a covenant of healing, but He gives you this warning: "Whoever breaks through a wall will be bitten by a serpent" (Eccl. 10:8). What is God saying? A wall speaks of protection. The Bible says if protection is broken, a demon will bite. What is your protection? The Word of the living God!

Do you want God's healing? Let the Word saturate your being. Let it dominate your heart, your mind, and your emotions. Love it, confess it, and obey it. If the Word becomes your whole life, it will totally surround you—on the left and the right, on the front and the back. The Word will be your protection and no serpent can bite you. But if that hedge is broken,

Satan and his demons will strike. And sickness is one result of that attack.

Scripture declares that "whoever has no rule over his own spirit / is like a city broken down, without walls" (Prov. 25:28). If you don't rule your life with the Word, there are no walls of protection surrounding you.

"Lord, Why Am I Sick?"

A man recently asked, "Benny, what happens if I fail and sickness enters my body?"

My answer did not change. "Stand on the Word," I told him. "Stand on the Word."

Years ago, one of America's greatest healing evangelists, William Branham, a man who had prayed for the deliverance of thousands, became sick. Lying there with a high fever, he cried out, "Lord, why am I sick? I have a meeting tonight and here I am lying on a bed of affliction. Lord, You are using me to bring healing to others. How embarrassing that I should walk on the platform a sick man. Heal me, Lord!"

The Lord would not answer.

"Heal me, Lord!" he said again.

Still no answer.

Suddenly, the Holy Spirit spoke and said, "The Word is health to all your flesh. The Word is health to all your flesh."

Branham began to recite Proverbs 4:22, but now he personalized the words: "The Word is health to all *my* flesh! The Word is health to all *my* flesh!"

Then he said, "Lord, if the Word is health to all my flesh, I will stand on Your Word that says 'concerning the work of My hands, you command Me'" (Isa. 45:11). The Lord did not say to "ask," He said "command Me." And that is what Branham did. God promised it and the evangelist commanded Him to do it. He said, "My God, I command in the name of Jesus that the Word will work for me!" And as he began commanding the Word to work, he arose from that bed and claimed his healing.

He said he still felt sick, but he refused to pay attention to the symptoms. Half an hour later the fever had gone, strength had poured into his being, and he walked to the platform that night a healthy man.

There's Healing in Worship

The prophet Jeremiah asked: "Is there no balm in Gilead, / Is there no physician there? / Why then is there no recovery / For the health of the daughter of my people?" (Jer. 8:22).

This Scripture contains a marvelous truth that holds a key to your healing. Jeremiah asks, "Is there no balm in Gilead?" The word *balm* in Hebrew speaks of healing. And the word *Gilead* speaks of worship. He is asking, "Is there no healing in worship?" Of course there is. And you need to act upon the knowledge that your worship brings healing.

If you confess the Word and nothing seems to happen, begin to worship the Lord God of heaven. Worship Him for His promises. Worship and say, "Jesus, You bore my sickness. I will not bear it. Thank You because Your Word says, 'By Your stripes I am healed.'" As you begin worshiping the Lord, you will watch healing come into your being.

What happened at Calvary can even protect you from pain.

In Old Testament times, if a person was sick he received a pain killer—myrrh. "A bundle of myrrh is my beloved to me, / That lies all night between my breasts" (Song 1:13).

When Christ was on the cross, He was offered myrrh. "Then they gave Him wine mingled with myrrh to drink, but He did not take it" (Mark 15:23). It was customary to give such a drink to a person being crucified so that he would not feel the pain.

Why did the Lord Jesus refuse it? Christ rejected the myrrh because He did not want to die without pain. He would die receiving all our anguish and torment. Christ is your "pain killer," the one on whom you call for assistance in your time of need. He will lie beside you in your darkest hour to stop the hurt and bring you healing.

The Lord is your shelter and your shield. He is your wall of protection.

Chapter 14

———— ✝ ————

A Harvest of Healing

God's law regarding sowing and reaping is clear. You will never celebrate the harvest unless you have carefully planted the seed and cared for the crop. This also applies to healing.

If you sow seeds of doubt and unbelief, your crop will be a failure. That is why your mentality must change. God wants you to plant with faith, hope, and love.

In the New Testament we read that "God anointed Jesus of Nazareth with the Holy Spirit and with power, who went about doing good and healing all who were oppressed by the devil, for God was with Him" (Acts 10:38). Again, the devil in this verse brings sickness, not God.

Instead of sowing seeds of doubt, look up to the Father and say, "God in heaven, You promised that healing is mine if I obey You. Now Lord, You know that I am not perfect, but the Word says that through Christ I am righteous."

You see, the law could never be totally obeyed under the Old Covenant. It was impossible. Jesus took your disobedience and fulfilled the law. For that reason, you and I can obey the laws of God. That is why you can pray with assurance, "Father, Your Word says that Jesus took my pain, my sickness, my sorrows, and my sin. Your Word says that I am the righteousness of God, despite my shortcomings, and that sickness does not belong in my body."

"My Body Won't Obey"

Recently a member of my congregation told me her story. She said, "When I was a child, I was treated badly by my parents and for years have been very sick." She went on to relate how she had been in and out of hospitals more times than she could remember, and that her physical problems continued to that very day.

Her reason for wanting to talk to me was that she wanted to tell me she had listened very carefully to my messages on healing. And everything I preach, she believes.

She said, "Pastor Hinn, I've done everything you've said. In some cases I began doing it even before you told me. I've been trying to practice God's Word for years. I have faith that God wants me healed. And I have trusted God to heal me as His Word promises. However, my miracle has not been manifested in a physical form. My body won't obey."

Then she looked at me with sorrow in her eyes and asked, "Why am I still sick?"

I said to the woman, "Let's imagine there is a line drawn across the floor. On one side of the line there are people with the wrong concept regarding God's Word and the wrong understanding of how God heals."

Then I said, "Now let's suppose a person crosses that line." Pointing to the imaginary line, I continued, "Healing doesn't necessarily happen here. There is all this space to walk on before you get it."

She asked, "What is that space?"

I responded, "When you sow a seed you can't expect to reap the harvest tomorrow. You've got to give the seed time to take root, to bear the fruit, and then you'll reap the harvest. I believe you have crossed over the line. You have entered the area where God can begin to do His work."

She said, "Pastor, you know that I should be dead by now. My doctors are amazed that I am still alive."

I told her, "You are alive because your faith is alive. You are trusting Him with every part of your being. Remember that 'faith is the substance of things hoped for, the evidence of things not seen.' Now give your body a chance to follow and allow the healing to be manifest. Don't give up! Your miracle is getting closer every day."

Crossing the Line

When will you receive your healing? Today? Tomorrow? The most important fact to know is that you received the provision for your healing two thousand years ago. It happened on the cross.

When you believe in your heart, soul, and mind that the atonement for your healing has already taken place, you have "crossed the line." You have entered the fertile ground where the seed can grow in good soil where God can produce a harvest.

God wants you to eliminate the negative, faith-shattering thoughts Satan would have you believe —doubts he attempts to plant in your mind. He wants you to say, "I will not accept or tolerate sickness and disease!"

What kind of seed should you sow? Jesus said, "The seed is the word of God" (Luke 8:11).

Never forget the words found in Proverbs: "My son, give attention to my words; / Incline your ear to my sayings. / Do not let them depart from your eyes; / Keep them in the midst of your heart; / For they are life to those who find them, / And health to all their flesh" (Prov. 4:20–22).

How does health come? Your healing comes through the Word. But it's not always automatic. Scripture tells us sometimes we have to find it. And how does that happen? Three ways. First, by being attentive. Second, by having a steadfast look. And third, by keeping the Word in your heart.

You will find, or "catch," the Word by having your ears open, your eyes open, and your heart open to it. Scripture does not say you will find healing with a little whisper, or with a glance, or with a little feeling from your heart. It takes bold, decisive action!

Paul wrote to the church at Rome, "Faith comes by hearing, and hearing by the word of God" (Rom. 10:17). One person said it this way: Faith comes by "hearing and hearing." In other words, we need to keep on hearing what God is saying and not rest on what we read or heard yesterday. You will never absorb the Word into your life by hearing it once. You need to hear, and hear, and hear again.

You also need to have a steadfast look. Keep looking, and looking, and looking. Then your heart must love it, and love it, and love it. This is how you will find—and sow—your healing.

God wants you to show diligence so that "you do not become sluggish, but imitate those who through faith and patience inherit the promises" (Heb. 6:12).

When the Word is sown, it's time for "faith and patience." When you plant the seed you have discovered, don't always expect it to bring forth life in twenty-four hours. Have both *assurance* and *endurance*. "Therefore do not cast away your confidence, which has great reward" (Heb. 10:35).

"He's Right on Time"

Plant your seed and keep watering it. You will never enjoy the abundance of your healing if you allow your field to become parched and dry. Continue to water your faith with the Word and never, never give up.

Yes, God wants you healed. But remember, it took a long time for you to become as you are. And it may take time for you to become a totally changed person. The Lord cleanses your heart in an instant at salvation, but being "transformed by the renewing of your mind" can be a longer journey. In the same way, your healing may take place over a period of time.

Have you crossed the line? Are you in a position for God to perform a miracle in your life? Don't give up on God.

Some people like to pick a favorite verse from Scripture and say, "If I'll just use that, God will heal me." They may quote again and again, "He was wounded for our transgressions, / He was bruised for our iniquities; / The chastisement for our peace was upon Him, / And by His stripes we are healed" (Isa. 53:5).

It is a powerful verse, but don't try to base God's healing power on just one Scripture. God says the Word must *saturate* you. Only then will "health come to your flesh." The Word of God from Genesis to Revelation needs to permeate your life. Remember, you've got to hear it and keep hearing it. See it and keep seeing it. Love it and keep loving it. The Word has the power to bring the healing for which you have prayed so long.

The Word works wonders. Paul said, "When you received the word of God which you heard from us, you welcomed it not as the word of men, but as it is in truth, the word of God, which also effectively works in you who believe" (1 Thess. 2:13).

Where Is Your Faith?

Some people, however, have faith in the wrong things. They have great difficulty believing that God will answer their prayers. They aren't sure the Word works, and it shows in their behavior.

Remember, what you sow, you will reap. If you plant seeds of unbelief, your harvest will be sad indeed. But if your field has been carefully sown with the Word, and with faith, your barns will be filled to overflowing. And if you are in need of God's touch, you will reap a harvest of healing.

Chapter 15

———— † ————

Claim Your Inheritance

Receiving a miracle is not something you earn by good works. Nor is it a gift to show love and appreciation. Healing belongs to you. It's your *inheritance* (Ex. 15:26).

Your road to health and recovery is clearly marked. Scripture says that the Word must first be "built" in you. And when that happens, you are ready to receive what is rightfully yours. "And now, brethren, I commend you to God and to the word of His grace, which is able to build you up and give you an inheritance among all those who are sanctified" (Acts 20:32).

In an age of fast foods, instant photography, and computer chips, people want everything *now*. And they expect the Lord to respond in the same way. But God's kingdom does not function with a microwave mentality. The Word first builds, then it gives.

Building takes time, and God's Word is what puts the pieces together. The word *build* as used here is the Greek word for "construction." It begins with a solid foundation at conversion and grows brick by brick, layer upon layer, until the structure becomes a masterpiece.

None of us like to wait. But if a farmer makes a meal from his seed, there will be nothing left to sustain him in the days ahead. He doesn't eat his seed. It is by planting the seed of truth that you will be set free.

You may be saying, "I'm still sick. I'm still miserable and defeated." Perhaps you wonder, "Lord, where is my health? My legs are hurting, my head is aching, my body is in constant pain." You may even conclude that the only thing worth rejoicing about is that you have been born again. Physically, you are in dire need.

Don't panic. You are on the right track. By being built up in the Word, you are planting seeds that will bring healing from your head to your toes.

As you walk the road hearing, seeing, and loving the Word, the process of building continues. Steady progress is being made day after day. Since you are so close to what is happening, you may not be able to measure your growth. Your spirit has been changed. Your soul is being changed. In Romans 12:1-2, the Scriptures tell us "I beseech you therefore, brethren, by the mercies of God, that you present your bodies a living sacrifice, holy, acceptable to God, which is your reasonable service. And do not be conformed to this world, but be transformed by the renewing of your mind, that you may prove what is that good and acceptable and perfect will of God." So, in the new birth your spirit was saved, your soul is being saved, and the body will be saved. In the same way, your spirit was healed at the cross, and your soul (emotions, intellect, and will) is healed as the Word develops in you. And one day you will see the transformation taking place in your body.

Suddenly you'll say, "It's happening. I feel better and different than I felt three weeks ago!" The transformation of the inner man takes place in an instant, but outward signs may take longer. The Word begins to present you with your inheritance deep on the inside. Before long your emotions are healed, and your mind begins to think as the Father thinks. It is a law of God and of nature that what happens on the inside will eventually affect the outside. The exterior will be touched by the overflow from the interior.

A Question of Faith

Give the Word time to pour its life into you and flood your body. Walk life's road saying, "The Word is being built within me. Through faith and patience I inherit the promises." His Word will give you strength and endurance, even when your spiritual legs are aching and you feel like giving up.

Allow the seed time to take root, to bring forth life, and to bear fruit. As you journey, God is looking for two important elements: faith and confession.

Is faith essential to healing? Absolutely. Your faith

must grow and increase daily if you want to receive your inheritance.

The Lord often healed when men and women approached Him in faith. At other times, being moved by compassion, the Lord Jesus healed without specifically being asked. And there were other times in the ministry of our Lord Jesus when it wasn't God's timing to heal.

I was recently asked, "Why didn't Jesus heal everyone who came near Him? He only healed certain ones and left many sick."

That is a good question. If the Lord walked through the Gate Beautiful many times, why did He not heal the man who had been sitting there who Peter and John healed? And what about the others at the gate who were crippled or blind and begging alms? Why was only *one* of them healed?

If you remember Acts 3:2, the Bible talks of this man sitting at the gate asking for alms. Verse 6 tells of the man's healing and, as a result, five thousand men were born again (Acts 4:4). I believe the glorious result of this miracle is the reason the man was healed at this time rather than earlier. God is the God of perfect timing, and this is a great example of His perfect will at work but also remember that God declared through Isaiah that His ways are not man's ways (Isa. 55:8). There will always be something we, as humans, won't know or understand. There will always be secret things that belong to God (Deut. 29:29).

In services of my own ministry, repeatedly the Holy Spirit has let me know that an individual has just been healed. How did it happen? I did not go to him and pray the prayer of faith. The Holy Spirit, knowing he was ready, touched him.

The element of faith as a key to healing is beyond explanation. Even though there will always be questions about healing and faith, we can be certain that faith is a key in God's healing process. What we do know is that it is necessary. Repeatedly, before Christ extended healing, He observed the person's faith—*He saw it*. In the New Testament, faith is often seen rather than heard.

At Capernaum, "they brought to Him a paralytic lying on a bed. And Jesus, seeing their faith, said to the paralytic, 'Son, be of good cheer; your sins are forgiven you'" (Matt. 9:2). He saw the faith of those men carrying the paralytic, and He was moved with compassion. Moments later, the man was totally healed but only after the man's sins were forgiven.

Furthermore, we have examples in Scripture where we find individuals approaching Jesus determined to be healed. The woman with the issue of blood was faced with the opposition of the crowds around Jesus. Yet she was so set on being healed, she released her faith, fought her way into Jesus' presence, touched His garment, and received her healing. In the early days of my ministry, God opened my eyes to this fact: People can receive miracles because they are determined to receive their inheritance.

"Lady, Sit Down!"

Several years ago in Phoenix, Arizona, while I was preaching, I noticed a commotion in the audience of several thousand people. I looked closely to see a woman in a wheelchair trying to stand up. Suddenly, she was holding on to the chair and began moving her legs from side to side.

I continued to preach, but it seemed that people everywhere were turning their attention to the lady—and I was no exception. I had not yet come to believe what I am teaching you now, and I thought, "That lady is going to fall and injure herself."

Immediately, I spoke to her from the platform and said, "Lady, sit down because God is not healing you."

As I continued my message, I glanced down and saw that once again she was trying to move her legs back and forth. It seemed she would not stop. I repeated "Please take your seat."

At the end of the service, while dozens of people came forward for salvation, I saw her again—out of her wheelchair, moving her legs, and now the wheelchair began to move from its position. As I was concerned that she might fall and hurt herself, I decided to get her back in that chair even if I had to force her to be seated.

By this time I was a little upset at all the distraction she had caused throughout my message. I walked over to her and said, "Lady, I told you during the entire service to stay in your wheelchair. You could fall and really hurt yourself."

Suddenly, with great excitement, she began to talk to me; every word was in Spanish. "Do you speak English?" I asked. But she continued to respond in her own language. She hadn't understood a word I had said that night. She probably thought I had been telling her that God was going to perform a miracle.

I called for an interpreter and said, "Tell her to sit down because God hasn't healed her. When she is healed, she can get up."

She got my message, and I got her response. Through the interpreter she said, "You tell that preacher that I am going to get healed tonight whether he likes it or not!"

I was stunned. I saw faith as I had never seen it. Immediately I took her by the hand and said, "In Jesus' name!" The moment I spoke His name the woman began to shout in Spanish! I didn't understand a word she said, but I felt God's presence as she spoke. Instantly, she jumped out of that wheelchair and took off. All I could do was to stand there looking at her in amazement. Across the entire auditorium people began to praise the Lord with a mighty voice.

It was a great lesson for me. The poor lady was trying to get a message to me, and I was too dense to see it! What was she doing? *She was exercising her faith.* I saw it and could not recognize it. But Jesus saw it.

I am certain that the Spanish lady had been convinced through the Word that God would heal her. I believe she had been built up through faith and patience, and this was her moment to reap the results. She exercised her faith and was waiting for me to exercise mine.

When you reach that place of readiness, you will hear the words of Jesus saying, "As you have believed, so let it be done for you" (Matt. 8:13).

Words of Power

Faith plays a vital role in healing, and so does confession.

You ask, "Why must I affirm the promises of God? Why is it so important?" Confession without the Holy Spirit is merely empty words. In Genesis 1:2 it declares "The earth was without form, and void; and darkness was on the face of the deep. And the Spirit of God was hovering over the face of the waters." Verse 3 goes on to say "Then God said, 'Let there be light'; and there was light." Imagine, God Himself didn't speak until the Holy Spirit moved. Speaking the Word of God without the movement of the Holy Spirit is useless. Psalm 91:1-2 speaks again of the importance of confession. "He who dwells in the secret place of the Most High / Shall abide under the shadow of the Almighty. / I will say of the Lord, 'He is my refuge and my fortress; / My God, in Him I will trust.'" Here we see that we must rest in God's presence to affirm His promises.

I have discovered that confession gives the lordship to your human spirit over your body and your mind. Scripture warns us, however, that "you are snared by the words of your own mouth" (Prov. 6:2). You are taken captive and dominated by your words, and so is your spirit.

It is important that the right words take authority in your life. You are to speak God's Word in total accord with the Father. To confess His promises is simply to agree aloud with Him.

You say, "I've tried that, but I haven't seen the results."

We need to grasp our confession tightly and not

let go. "Seeing then that we have a great High Priest who has passed through the heavens, Jesus the Son of God, let us hold fast our confession" (Heb. 4:14). The Word tells us to "hold fast the confession of our hope without wavering, for He who promised is faithful" (Heb. 10:23).

In Romans 10:10 we read, "With the mouth confession is made to salvation." And that is where many people stop. They believe it is only meant for the time you profess that Jesus is Lord.

We are instructed to "acknowledge" our faith, "confess it," and "hold it fast." Even the psalmist talked about it. "Whoever offers praise glorifies Me; / And to him who orders his conduct aright / I will show the salvation of God" (Ps. 50:23). Your conversation must be in line with the Word. And when it is, you will see His salvation.

However your words alone, apart from the moving of the Holy Spirit in your heart, will not in themselves produce your inheritance.

Confession gives God's authority to your spirit and you will know God's healing power.

Why should you keep confessing? Because God is faithful to His promises. When you see the promise far ahead, that is the time to confess it, believe it, walk it, see it, and love it. Let the Word fill you and build you. And one day soon you will receive your inheritance.

Chapter 16

———————— † ————————

Farewell to Fear

God does not promise that the road to your miracle will be smooth. The path is filled with roadblocks and detours of every description.

Without question you will face one of hell's most destructive forces. It came against the disciples and the followers of Jesus. And it will come against you.

What will become your greatest challenge? *Fear*— Satan's greatest tool.

The moment you begin living and acting on faith and on the Word, you will be a target for attack. Fear will come as surely as the sun will rise. You can count on it. The question is not whether it will come, but how you will deal with it.

The devil has no intention of leaving you alone, especially when you walk by faith. He will try to strike at you with every ounce of his evil energy. The more you do for God the more Satan will attack you.

"It's Something You See"

He will come against you just as he harassed Abraham.

God made Abraham a promise that he would be forever favored. He said, "I will make you a great nation; / I will bless you / And make your name great; / And you shall be a blessing. / I will bless those who bless you, / And I will curse him who curses you; / And in you all the families of the earth shall be blessed" (Gen. 12:2–3).

Abraham, the "father of faith," came face to face with the destructive force we are talking about— fear. He collapsed with fright, and God had to correct him.

The Lord said, "Do not be afraid, Abram. I am your shield, your exceedingly great reward" (Gen. 15:1). Fear can thwart God's protection. The Lord was saying "If you fear, I will not be your shield."

What was he fearing? God promised Abraham that he would have children and be the father of many nations. Now he was worried that he would have no children. "Lord GOD, what will You give me, seeing I go childless? . . . You have given me no offspring" (vv. 2–3).

Fear, like faith, is something you see. It's a picture. Abraham saw himself childless and became frightened. That is why God corrected him.

Abraham was in his tent, gripped with anxiety and fear. God told him to get up and go outside. It was night and the Lord told him, "'Look now toward heaven, and count the stars if you are able to number them.' And He said to him, 'So shall your descendants be'" (Gen. 15:5).

God wanted Abraham to start counting stars because *faith is a picture.* Then the Lord changed the picture for Abraham from stars to children. He was saying, "Stop seeing yourself with nothing, and see yourself with a multitude. See your offspring. See your future!"

When Abraham wasn't counting stars, he was counting grains of sand. God told him, "I will multiply your descendants as the stars of the heaven and as the sand which is on the seashore; and your descendants shall possess the gate of their enemies" (Gen. 22:17).

"One, Two, Three"

God took away Abraham's "fear picture" and commanded him to see a "faith picture." He must have counted for a long, long time. For fourteen long years what do you think Abraham did? He counted the stars and the sand. Why? Because fear kept coming against him, clouding his vision. Proverbs 29:18 (KJV) cautions us that where there is no vision the people perish. Fear does not run and hide, nor does the devil take a vacation.

Can you see Abraham as fear came upon him, counting, "One, two, three, four, five"? He probably walked with a bucket full of sand. And at night he counted as he scanned the heavens.

Without question, fear is the most destructive tool of Satan. Scripture tells us that hell will be crowded because of it. "But the fearful, and unbelieving, . . . shall have their part in the lake which burneth with fire and brimstone: which is the second death" (Rev. 21:8 KJV).

With fear being such a powerful force, it becomes easy to understand why more people do not receive their healing. A list of people's apprehensions would fill volumes.

Recently, at a service in our church, a man was miraculously healed. There was no question concerning what the Lord did for him. But I was shaken when he came to me a few days later and said, "I'm afraid I am going to get sick again."

"Don't say that," I cautioned him. "Erase the words 'I'm afraid' from your mind and from your lips." I told him to "stop seeing yourself sick and see yourself healed!"

"Keep on Counting"

I believe it is much more difficult to count stars and sand for fourteen years than to believe God for the healing of your body. People must have called Abraham "crazy." But when his son was born, God said, "That's one! Keep on counting."

Today, Abraham must look down from heaven and say, "Look at that multitude. It is still growing. Stars are still being added."

Stop considering the barriers that surround you. Start believing the Word. Start seeing and counting the stars.

Glowing on the Sea

After the Lord Jesus miraculously fed five thousand on the shore of the Sea of Galilee, late in the afternoon, He asked His disciples to leave so He could have some time alone. "Immediately Jesus made His disciples get into the boat and go before Him to the

other side, while He sent the multitudes away"
(Matt. 14:22). Then, "He went up on a mountain by
Himself to pray. And when evening had come, He
was alone there" (v. 23).

He prayed for ten to twelve hours, until the
"fourth watch," which was early in the morning
when it was still dark. We all know what happened
next. The disciples' boat was in the middle of the
sea, being tossed about by a great storm. Jesus came
to them, walking on the water.

Perhaps the greatest miracle was not that Christ
walked on the sea, but that the disciples could see
Him in the dark, and in the storm. How do you think
they saw Him? I believe that, after praying for ten
hours on the mountain, the Lord was actually shining. There was a beam of light coming toward the
boat. Jesus was glowing with the glory of God!

"And when the disciples saw Him walking on the
sea, they were troubled, saying, 'It is a ghost!' And
they cried out for fear" (v. 26).

The Lord called to them, saying, "Be of good
cheer! It is I; do not be afraid" (v. 27). But Peter
wasn't sure it was Jesus. He said, "'Lord, if it is You,
command me to come to You on the water.' So He
said, 'Come.' And when Peter had come down out
of the boat, he walked on the water to go to Jesus"
(vv. 28–29).

I don't believe Peter tested the water. He stepped
out of that boat and started walking. What he was
walking on was not the water. I believe he was
walking on the Word that said, "Come!"

But as Peter was walking toward the bright glow
of Christ, suddenly he felt a wind pass by him. He

panicked with fear. The Bible says, "When he saw that the wind was boisterous, he was afraid; and beginning to sink he cried out, saying, 'Lord, save me!'" (v. 30).

It was dark and he probably could not see the water too well. How could he "see" the wind? He saw it in his mind. It was a *fear picture*. He had been walking in faith, but he felt the wind and visualized disaster. What happened? Peter began to sink.

He cried, "'Lord, save me.' And immediately Jesus stretched out His hand and caught him, and said to him, 'O you of little faith, why did you doubt?'" (vv. 30–31). Peter was so shaken that he did not answer. They stepped into the boat, the wind ceased, and they crossed safely to the other side.

The Lord taught Peter a powerful lesson. Anything is possible when faith is exercised. But when "Come!" was replaced by the wind and the storm, he began to sink.

Instead of having an anxiety attack, start counting your stars, confessing His promises, and walking toward the Lord Jesus.

Say "Farewell!" to fear.

Chapter 17

✝

Forever Healed

I have frequently been asked, "Pastor Hinn, how can I keep my healing?" Others have wanted to know, "Why do some people lose their healing?" These are both important questions because I firmly believe the Lord wants you to be healed completely, and permanently.

What you have been reading should make it clear that the Word of God is the key that unlocks the door to your healing. Some may wonder, "Do I have to be a Bible scholar to be a candidate for God's touch?" Not at all. Even a new Christian can receive the Lord's healing power, and there are millions of testimonies that prove it.

God is sovereign. He can grant healing when, where, and to whom He chooses. But the moment a person is healed, he should begin to immerse himself in the Word without delay. The continuance of his healing depends on it. The psalmist wrote, "I will never forget Your precepts, / For by them You have given me life" (Ps. 119:93).

God's Word quickens you and keeps you alive. That's why it is vital for you to be constantly filled with the life of the Father, and not with the destructive forces of Satan. "His divine power has given to us all things that pertain to life and godliness, through the knowledge of Him who called us by glory and virtue" (2 Peter 1:3).

How do you get that knowledge of Him? Through His Word.

When God's knowledge permeates you, His divine power and life leave no room for sicknesses. The Word remains alive as you read it, hear it, and associate with those who love it. That is why it is important to stay in the atmosphere of the Word.

There is a great difference between eating a hamburger and fries at a fast-food restaurant and enjoying a healthy meal with your family around the dining room table. The environment makes the difference, not to mention the great improvement in nutrition.

It is vital that you find a church that gives you the meat of God's Word. Both your spiritual and your physical health are at stake.

Yours to Keep

The Lord not only wants you to receive your healing, He wants it to continue. Here are seven specific ways you can keep your healing.

1. *Trust in God.* "Cursed is the man who trusts in man / And makes flesh his strength, / Whose heart departs from the LORD" (Jer. 17:5). Those are harsh

and negative words, but they are true. Then we read: "Blessed is the man who trusts in the LORD, / And whose hope is the LORD" (v. 7).

Those words are followed by the promise of healing. "For he shall be like a tree planted by the waters, / Which spreads out its roots by the river, / And will not fear when heat comes; / But her leaf will be green, / And will not be anxious in the year of drought, / Nor will cease from yielding fruit" (v. 8). God says that if you will trust Him, you will stay healed.

2. *Keep His Word.* The advice found in Proverbs is worth committing to memory. "My son, give attention to my words; / Incline your ear to my sayings. / Do not let them depart from your eyes; / Keep them in the midst of your heart; / For they are life to those who find them, / And health to all their flesh" (Prov. 4:20–22).

3. *Confess your faults one to another.* Healing requires more than an anointing with oil. The words of James make it clear. "Is anyone among you sick? Let him call for the elders of the church, and let them pray over him, anointing him with oil in the name of the Lord. And the prayer of faith will save the sick, and the Lord will raise him up. And if he has committed sins, he will be forgiven. Confess your trespasses to one another, and pray for one another, that you may be healed. The effective, fervent prayer of a righteous man avails much" (James 5:14–16).

4. *Speak God's language.* "There is one who speaks like the piercings of a sword, but the tongue of the wise promotes health" (Prov. 12:18). If you

expect to live in complete health, you must learn to speak what God speaks. "He who guards his mouth preserves his life" (Prov. 13:3).

5. *Stay in prayer.* "He who dwells in the secret place of the Most High / Shall abide under the shadow of the Almighty" (Ps. 91:1). The "secret place" is prayer. "I will say of the LORD, 'He is my refuge and my fortress; / My God, in Him I will trust.' / Surely He shall deliver you from the snare of the fowler / And from the perilous pestilence. / He shall cover you with His feathers, / And under His wings you shall take refuge; / His truth shall be your shield and buckler" (vv. 2–4).

The psalmist then presents a tremendous promise. "No evil shall befall you, / Nor shall any plague come near your dwelling; / For He shall give His angels charge over you, / To keep you in all your ways" (vv. 10–11).

Prayer keeps you in health.

6. *Resist the devil.* "Therefore submit to God. Resist the devil and he will flee from you. Draw near to God and He will draw near to you" (James 4:7–8). How do you push Satan away? By submitting to the Lord.

7. *Observe the laws of nature.* Why should the Lord continue to grant healing if you violate His rules of good health? "Do you not know that you are the temple of God and that the Spirit of God dwells in you? If anyone defiles the temple of God, God will destroy him. For the temple of God is holy, which temple you are" (1 Cor. 3:16–17).

By keeping these seven rules of healing, you can know continued health and life.

What Are You Eating?

The Word of the Lord is precise concerning the foods we place in our bodies. In the law of Moses, the Lord gave Jews rules regarding eating, but many people laugh at these ordinances as old-fashioned and irrelevant.

At the risk of being misunderstood, I want to share my personal beliefs regarding foods we should and should not eat.

You may think I am "old-fashioned," or out of touch with reality, but I do not eat food which the Bible forbids.

You might say, "Benny, you were born in Israel where they don't eat certain things." That is not the reason. It's not cultural. I am not telling you what is right for you, but to me the Word is the Word. If it tells me not to eat it, I don't.

Isn't it amazing that nutritional experts and medical doctors are now telling people to eat many of the same foods that God commanded Moses to instruct the children of Israel to eat? What the church would not believe for years the world is now embracing.

Discovery after discovery tells us that certain foods cause cancer. Yet for hundreds of years people have ignored what God said to Moses, and their bodies have suffered.

Why do I stick to "Bible foods"? The argument may be weak spiritually, but when you look around, it is not. You may disagree, but I only share this out of love and concern. I do not want you or your family to suffer with sickness because of your eating habits.

God can heal you right now, but you will not keep your health if you take into your body something of which I believe He disapproves. For example, I do not eat rare meat. God said that we must not eat blood. You say, "If it's not in the New Testament, I won't listen."

James said to the Council at Jerusalem, "I judge that we should not trouble those from among the Gentiles who are turning to God, but that we write to them to abstain from things polluted by idols, from sexual immorality, from things strangled, and from blood" (Acts 15:19–20).

God spoke much on the topic of food. Did you know that if all the passages in Scripture regarding food were placed together, they would make one of the longest books of the Bible?

Some people attempt to find one verse that would negate hundreds of Scriptures regarding God's laws of health. But I believe *all* His teaching is there for a purpose.

You may disagree, but I believe I have an obligation to the Father to eat His healthy foods. And I have decided to live by His rules.

Without being legalistic about it, I sincerely believe following God's dietary plan is the healthiest way for me to eat. I also believe that we need to be careful of the chemicals we allow to enter our bodies through the processed and treated foods we eat. Dear friends, please don't misunderstand me here. I love each of you and only want you to take seriously what you eat and consider that God's Word does speak extensively about our eating healthy foods. Take a look at the Scriptures for yourself. Consider what you are eating and then make your own decisions.

Now a brief word about exercise. In addition to good eating habits, I'm convinced a regular exercise plan is another way we can stay healthy. Regardless of your age, or the shape you are in, there is some kind of exercise which is right for you.

I try to do some exercise every day, and I always feel better when I do. God blessed us with brains and it sure makes sense to me to use them. In addition to taking care of ourselves spiritually through Scripture reading, worship, and confession, I know God wants each of us to take care of ourselves physically through proper diet and exercise.

The Lord wants us to live a long, fruitful, and healthy life. Healing is a vital provision of God's covenant with us. I encourage you to commit yourselves today to a daily walk with our Lord Jesus. Let's enjoy the benefits of a healthy life and confess God's provision for healing when sickness invades our world. You can claim God's provision for healing right this moment and trust in His promise to restore you to health (Jer. 30:17).

Part Three

The Miracles
God Provided

Chapter 18

———— † ————

I'm Soaring Now

To me, the miracle-working power of the Lord is not a subject for debate. I'll leave that to the critics, the doubters, the skeptics, and those who have never experienced God's healing touch.

I only know that for years I had a severe problem with stuttering, and suddenly I was totally healed.

But what about Lynn Whitmore in Knoxville? She had lost her sight in one eye and was losing vision in the other because of irreversible damage to the optic track. Was it possible that God could somehow heal her?

What would happen to Dick Gadd in Myrtle Beach with a deformed hand and cancer in his back? Was there hope for Marsha Brantley in Oklahoma whose body was being tortured by the effects of lupus? And what was the future of Charlie McLain in Tulsa who was strapped to a tube-feeding machine, and too weak for another surgery on his blocked intestine?

Sarah Knapp, the nurse in Illinois, was still suffering with severe pain in her arm and shoulder. Little Timothy Mercer in Orlando, who was born with hypoplastic lungs, continued to fight for his life.

Doreen Maddeaux in Toronto was facing yet another heart surgery. And what would happen to Dave Lane, the horse-breeder in Tennessee, who was diagnosed with a baseball-size malignant tumor in his colon?

Kathie's Intolerable Life

Kathie McGahuey was still in Milwaukie, Oregon, suffering from an extreme case of anaphylactic reactions and "environmental illness." She was hypersensitive to a countless list of odors, foods, and chemicals that made life almost intolerable. Most of her hair had fallen out.

When Kathie's ordeal began she weighed 250 pounds. Eleven years later her illness had reduced her to 110. "I had lost a whole person," she says.

When our television program began airing in Oregon in 1990, Kathie started to watch it. "It seemed that day after day my faith became stronger and stronger when I saw what the Lord was doing in the lives of others," said Kathie. "I prayed, read the Word, and believed God for my miracle."

When the announcement was made that we had scheduled a crusade in Portland, Kathie's expectations began to soar. "I believed with all my heart that the Lord was going to heal me in one of those meetings."

On July 25, 1991, the first day of the crusade, Kathie had another serious attack, but she was not about to let that stop her from attending the opening service. She and her husband, Kenneth, drove to the auditorium.

Kathie not only believed in healing, she believed in the Healer. "Although I was sick, people would come to our home to receive ministry," she says. "They would sit on the side of my bed and I would share the Word with them. It kept me from being depressed and self-centered. I knew I should not be focusing on my own problems."

Trying to Concentrate

At the Portland crusade the McGahueys were sitting toward the front of the packed auditorium. Kathie specifically sat in the back row of the section so she would not be penned in by odors. "The room was fairly large and there wasn't anywhere to go to get away from the smells," she says. "I sat as quietly as I could. I closed my eyes so I could concentrate on the Spirit of God through the praise and worship. I did not want anything to distract me."

Kathie was praying for a miracle, but she had a difficult time being specific. "Through the years I had been diagnosed with so many illnesses, I didn't know where to begin," she says. Any one of the disorders would have devastated the average person. Doctors had told her that her problems were the result of everything from a blood disorder to mercury poisoning. That night Kathie told the Lord, "Everything I have and everything I am is yours."

As the service continued I began to pray that the

Lord would honor the faith of those who needed a miracle. At that moment, something supernatural happened to Kathie.

"Suddenly the power of God hit me so strongly that I could feel it in the lower part of my stomach," she says. "It moved up into my chest and into my mouth; my teeth and my tongue felt numb."

People who were seated around her began to ask what was happening. "I couldn't speak," says Kathie. "All I could do was cry."

When we began to ask for those to come forward who had received a healing, the Lord began to speak to Kathie. "I heard a voice inside me say, 'If you don't stand up and go forward, you're going to lose what I've begun,'" she recalls.

To that point in the service, Kathie found it difficult to stay in the building because she was so weak and emaciated. She could only describe it by saying, "I felt there were many forces coming against me. I wanted to run and escape from all the smells."

The moment she started to stand, however, something remarkable happened. "It felt as though someone reached under my armpits and gently lifted me up," she recalls. "And when I stepped out into the aisle I don't even remember touching the floor— even though I know I did."

Kathie walked forward to an area near the platform and told some of the counselors and a medical doctor what she felt had happened. They wanted to be sure the healing had truly taken place. "As a test, they sprayed perfume on me, to see if there would be some kind of a reaction. Perhaps I should say they *poured* it on me, because that is what they did," Kathie says. "Normally, that would have sent my system into shock, but nothing happened."

A few minutes later, Kathie walked up the stairs of the platform to testify publicly of the healing that had taken place. I felt led of the Lord to tell her, "Within ninety days your hair will be back. You'll be gaining weight."

Another "First"

After the service, the McGahueys drove home rejoicing at what had taken place. "That night I went to bed and slept from a little after midnight until 3:30 A.M. When I woke up, nothing had happened—which was unusual," she says. "Normally, from being around odors, my colon would purge, I would vomit, go into anaphylactic shock and perhaps end up in the hospital."

When Kathie's eyes opened that night, the Lord spoke to her and said, "I'm going to begin your testimony now." She couldn't go back to sleep. "I believe He woke me up to show me that there had been no reaction to what I was exposed to that night. I was a new person."

When Kathie returned to the crusade the next day, she began to experience what would become a series of "firsts" for her. "I went into a public restroom by myself for the first time in years," she says. "I had to avoid such places because of my reaction to hair spray or cleaning solutions. When I walked out the door I was smiling—as thrilled as a little child with a new toy."

From the moment of her healing, Kathie's body

has grown stronger week by week. "Even though the healing of my allergic reactions was instant, my body was so emaciated that it has taken time to build up," she says. "A person does not go from starvation to a healthy weight overnight."

Once again Kathie can drive an automobile, work in the yard, and do things many people take for granted. "Every day is a new adventure for me," she says. "I weep and weep for joy because now I can attend church and I don't have to exit quickly when someone walks in with fabric softener on their clothing—or when someone is wearing a leather jacket."

After so many years of running from her environment, Kathie has had to retrain herself not to automatically react and retreat. "Even after being healed, my first response to the slightest hint of an odor was to leave the room as fast as possible," she says. "I had to force myself to sit down and remember that the environment was no longer going to plague me. It is as though I have been resurrected and the graveclothes have been taken off."

"Something Has Happened!"

Although she received her healing in one of our crusades, Kathie understands how God performs miracles. "I am grateful for a ministry like Pastor Hinn's, but I know that he is not my source. Jesus is my source," she explains. "I realize that God uses people, and that He will allow you to be in a certain place at a certain time, where there is a specific anointing."

After her healing, Kathie couldn't wait to go back

to her doctor. She took her husband with her. "Before the doctor even examined me, he said, 'Something has happened to you. What is it?'" Her husband just beamed.

Says Kathie, "I was sitting on the examining table and I told him what happened. And when he checked me, I was even more thrilled. He could find nothing wrong."

Even the woman who had been her hairdresser for seven years knew something had happened. She had seen Kathie's hair fall out and return nearly white in color. "After her miracle, her hair has almost completely darkened over three-fourths of her head." And she added, "As a licensed hairdresser I have never seen anyone's hair turn back to its natural color without it being dyed."

Her doctor says, "It's not only a miracle that this lady is still alive, but that she has recovered to the degree she has. Since July 1991, there has been a remarkable improvement. Kathie is no longer sensitive to smells, her diet is no longer completely restricted, her face has cleared up with respect to the quality of the complexion. It is my opinion that a miraculous healing is taking place."

After taking their first out–of–town trip together in more than eleven years, Kathie says, "My husband has a new wife." Kathie and Kenneth recently celebrated their twenty-fifth wedding anniversary.

Because of the pollution of the environment, the illness Kathie suffered has been called "a sickness of our time." As she says, "They call us the 'canaries' of society because of the endless testing they have done to people like us. In the olden days they would put a caged canary in a coal mine to determine if there was any deadly gas."

After her miracle, Kathie said, "Lord, I'm no longer a little canary; I am an eagle. I'm soaring now."

She told the Lord, "If You can do it for me, You can do it for anyone."

Chapter 19

✝

"Here, Read This"

There was no hope that Lynn Whitmore, in Knoxville, Tennessee, would ever see out of her right eye. According to her doctor, the blindness caused by pressure on her optic track was irreversible. And now the sight in her left eye was fading fast.

Losing her sight was only one of Lynn's problems. Her body was filled with intense pain and torment. "Please help me, Lord," she prayed.

In December 1991 Lynn and her adopted mother drove from their home in eastern Tennessee to Mobile, Alabama, where we were conducting a crusade.

"All the way down there I felt something wonderful was going to happen," she says. "I must confess, however, that since I was told that my blindness was permanent, I didn't pray for the miracle of sight. I knew that just wouldn't happen."

Lynn's prayer was that the Lord would take care of the pain in her body.

During the service, Lynn and her mother were in the choir. "We thought we'd get a better seat if we volunteered to sing," she said.

As usual in our crusades, during the first part of the service the lights in the auditorium were out, except for a spotlight on the platform where I was singing a duet with one of our soloists, Steve Brock.

Recalls Lynn, "It was the first crusade meeting I had ever attended. What I was seeing, even with my limited vision, was thrilling and exciting."

She Saw Angels

Lynn Whitmore says that she is not a person who has visions or other unusual spiritual experiences. That night, however, standing in the choir, she says, "I saw two angels with golden vials in their hands. They were huge angels." She turned to her mother and said, "I see angels pouring gold glitter from vials over the top of Benny and Steve Brock."

Her mother said, "Oh, that is wonderful. Where is it happening?"

Lynn said, "Right over there. They are in the air, hovering over both of them."

Then Lynn turned and exclaimed, "Mom! I can see it with my blind eye!"

When she looked back to the platform the angels she had seen were gone but her eye was healed. The intense pain was gone, too.

She could hardly wait to get back to Tennessee for another eye exam. "My doctor almost freaked out," she recalls. "He said, 'This isn't supposed to happen.'"

Lynn told him, "It did. It really did!"

His response was, "I can tell"—as Lynn continued reading the letters on the eye chart. The only thing she could not do was tell the difference between the O's and the G's on the last line.

She recalls what happened next. "My eye doctor put up a new chart because he thought perhaps I was playing a trick and had memorized the letters."

Then the doctor picked up a medical journal on his desk and said, "Here, read this."

"He placed something like a spatula over my good eye, and I began to read," she recalls. "Some of the technical words were beyond my comprehension, but I was reading every word on the page and spelling those I couldn't pronounce."

The report of the ophthalmologist on January 13, 1992, said, "Right eye 20/30 +2, Left eye 20/30 +2."

What would have happened if the Lord had not healed Lynn Whitmore? "The doctors told me I would have gone totally blind," she says.

Lynn believes in miracles.

Chapter 20

✝

"You're Going To Florida!"

Dick Gadd was not sure what to do next. His reconstructive bladder surgery had been a success, but now, in February 1992, he was at home in Myrtle Beach with a hand that was deformed from the complications. And now this. He was diagnosed with cancer in his back.

The previous summer, however, something unusual began to unfold. A few days after the initial diagnosis of tumors on Dick's bladder, the phone rang late at night. Dick's younger brother, John, was calling from Elkins, West Virginia. "We want you to know that we're praying for you," he told Dick's wife, Judy. Then he asked, "Have you ever heard of the services conducted by Benny Hill?"

"Do you mean Benny Hinn?" Judy asked.

"Yes, that's his name. A friend of mine told me about him."

Dick and Judy had seen our television program on a few occasions. John said, "If Dick will go, I will drive him to one of the services."

The next morning, Sherry, Judy's niece, arrived at the Gadds' home along with her husband. They had driven all night from West Virginia just to pray for Dick. Sherry handed Dick a shopping bag filled with cassette tapes. "You really need to listen to these messages," she said. "They are from a minister in Florida named Benny Hinn."

The couple stayed only about two hours and drove back home.

That fall, in November 1991, Kim Eidell, a young woman Dick and Judy had never met, called from West Virginia to say she had heard about Dick's condition from family members. Kim said she was praying with Dick for his healing. In March 1992, Kim called from Dick's mother's home and said, "We're all coming to Myrtle Beach, and we are going to drive with you to Florida to the Orlando Christian Center."

Because of his deteriorating condition, Gadd wasn't too sure about making the journey, but the woman said, "You don't have a choice. You're going to Florida!"

Dick says, "Since the name of this ministry had been coming up so often, Judy and I decided to go." Eleven people in two vans made the trip to Orlando on the weekend of March 21, 1992.

She Took His Hand

"We attended the Sunday morning service. I had never experienced anything like it," recalls Gadd. "It certainly was different than any Methodist or Baptist church I had attended."

On Sunday night, Dick, Judy, and their friends were seated on about the third row of the auditorium. "That was the first time I had ever raised my hands to the Lord in church. My inhibitions seemed to disappear," Dick says.

The service was almost over, and Dick was beginning to think it was not his night to receive a miracle.

After I finished preaching that night, I said to the congregation, "We are going to pray for God to heal you tonight. If you need healing, I want you to place your hand on that portion of your body that needs to be healed."

Dick placed his hand on his back. Judy reached over and gently held his deformed hand. "As Pastor Hinn was praying, I felt a cloud come over me and envelope my entire body from the top of my head to the bottom of my feet," says Gadd.

Dick walked to the front of the auditorium where a large group of people had gathered for prayer. Dick was standing with his hands raised to heaven when an usher asked him, "Did you receive a healing?"

Gadd answered, "I'm not sure, but something happened." Then he told the usher of how a white cloud had surrounded him like a pillow case.

"What was your problem?" the man asked.

"Well, I had cancer in my back," said Dick.

The usher took Gadd straight to the platform. Before I could pray for Dick, God's powerful anointing touched him, and he fell prostrate before the Lord. "Nothing like that had ever happened to me," Dick recalls.

After the service, the Gadds and their friends went to a restaurant to talk about the meeting, not fully comprehending what had happened. During the conversation, Judy turned to Dick and said, "Let me see your hand."

Dick was so busy discussing the service he thought, "Don't bother me; I'm talking."

But after two more requests from his wife, Dick placed his hand on the table. "We both looked at my hand in total amazement. The fingers were no longer curled, nor were they spread apart. My hand was totally healed," Dick says.

The Radiology Report

The Gadds rejoiced all the way back to Myrtle Beach. "I know I'm completely healed," Dick said. "There is no need to go back to the doctor." Then he added, "Why do I need to put God to the test?" Dick did not believe the Lord would heal his hand and leave a cancer to destroy him.

Several months later, on October 7, 1992, Gadd was involved in an automobile accident. "I was rear-ended by a Lincoln," he says. "After an x ray, the doctors thought I should have an MRI to check the damaged vertebrae. Since my automobile insurance would pay for it, I agreed to the test."

Gadd prayed, "Lord, don't let anything show up. Use the tests to glorify Your name."

The day after the tests, the doctor called Gadd and said, "I have good news for you. The mass is gone. It's hard to explain since cancer doesn't behave like this."

The radiology report says, "The soft tissue mass previously noted associated with the T8 and T9 vertebral bodies is no longer apparent. Also, the signal characteristics in these vertebral bodies has changed and is not currently compatible with malignancy."

"That's medical talk to describe a miracle," says Dick.

The future for the Gadds has changed drastically. Instead of worrying about the future, Dick and Judy are sharing their story of God's restoring power every day. Dick has returned to work; he is building and selling new homes.

Once again, Dick and Judy took a walk on the sands of Myrtle Beach. She put her hand in his and said, "You're right. Life doesn't get much better than this."

Chapter 21

———— † ————

A New Marsha

In Broken Arrow, Oklahoma, Marsha Brantley's ordeal with lupus, Raynaud's, Sjögren's syndrome, and ankylosing spondylitis, had left her in agonizing pain. Most of the time she walked with a cane and was often forced to use a wheelchair.

Marsha had suffered with pain since she was eighteen months old, but her problem was not officially diagnosed until 1989. The doctors offered little hope and she prayed for God to heal her. "The Lord let me know that I would be healed," she says. "I just did not know when or how."

Her sister-in-law heard about an October 1991 crusade we would be conducting in Tulsa. She told Marsha, "I believe you are going to be healed in those meetings."

Says Marsha, "I had never heard of Benny Hinn. I didn't know anything about a Miracle Crusade. I just thanked her for her prayers."

Marsha was raised in a church that did not preach healing. She recalls that "a month before the crusade, my pastor preached a message that all healings were psychosomatic and that there was no documentation for any so-called miracles."

Marsha didn't accept that.

Standing in the Sun

Since Marsha could no longer drive, her father-in-law offered to take her to the crusade on Friday, October 18. "When we arrived at the auditorium, I was amazed at the huge crowds waiting to get inside," she recalls. "Since my father-in-law was with me, I decided not to take my wheelchair. That was a mistake."

The crowds were so large that Marsha had to stand in line for about three hours while her father-in-law helped to hold her up and shade her from the hot sun. "I could feel my temperature rising," she says.

When the doors finally opened and they went inside, Marsha was in a great deal of pain and was crying. "But he would not let me sit down," she says. "We walked from one section to another. He was determined to get me as close to the front as possible. Fortunately, we were allowed to sit in a special section that had been reserved for the deaf."

During the service that night, the Lord impressed upon me that several people were being healed of specific ailments. At one point I said, "A blood disease is being healed."

Marsha Brantley claimed that for the lupus in her shoulders.

When I said, "A circulatory disease is being

healed," she claimed that for the Raynaud's. And I said, "There is someone here with a shoulder pain. It is leaving."

"At that moment," says Marsha, "all the agony in my shoulder just vanished. The only suffering that remained in my body was in my right hip. Then, a couple of minutes later, Pastor Hinn said, 'There is a person with a hip pain. The pain is now leaving your hip.'"

That must have been for Marsha, too. "I could move my hip. Miraculously, the hurting was gone. I was left with a feeling of total peace and was finally free of all my pain. It was wonderful," she says.

Marsha walked by herself over to an area where people were giving their testimonies. "A lady asked me to bend over," she remembers. "I touched my toes. It was the first time I had been able to do that since my high school days."

Later, when Marsha and her family watched a video of that meeting, she heard me say, "A bone disease is being healed," but by that time she was already giving her testimony and praising the Lord.

Painting the House

When Marsha arrived at her home late that night, it was a time of celebration. "My family had me running around the house, demonstrating what the Lord had done," she says.

Almost daily Marsha found that she could do things she never thought possible. "The last time I painted my mother's house was in 1988, and I could just barely hold the brush," she says. "It took me what seemed like forever to paint the inside walls.

But after my healing I painted her house again and was rejoicing and praising the Lord because there was no pain at all."

When she was examined after her healing, the physician wrote, "On October 18, Marsha went to a camp meeting. She had some form of sensation of change in her body during prayer. Since that time she has had sensations of warmth through her body; her back does not hurt anymore. Her energy is good. She feels well. Her Raynaud's is gone. She noticed no change when she discontinued her medication. Her exam is normal except for some hyperpigmentation left over from the plaquenil. I have never seen her with warm pink fingers before."

Although Marsha Brantley had a tremendous physical miracle, she says, "I also received an even greater spiritual miracle. There is a new hunger in my heart for God's Word. I experience the joy of the Lord in my spirit and know what it means to have a peace that passes understanding."

Says Marsha, "I'm a brand new person. I know from experience that the Lord does not want His people to live in sickness. He wants them to be healed."

If the Lord can heal Marsha, He can heal you.

Chapter 22

---------- † ----------

"Charlie! Look at Me!"

Charlie McLain was too weak to face another surgery. The Tulsa, Oklahoma, mortgage and loan officer had survived cancer, but the massive radiation treatments had literally fused his intestines together. Now there was a major blockage in the intestine.

The emergency operation on Christmas Eve 1990, his second in just two weeks, was a failure. Charlie was near death when they sent him home hooked to an IV. The doctors hoped that somehow he would gain enough strength so they could operate again.

"They told me the only hope was either to do a bypass on my intestinal tract, or remove my intestine altogether," he recalls. Charlie didn't want any part of that. He told them, "Get me home, and I'll be healed."

Is This Really You?

On Friday evening, February 1, 1991, McLain was stretched out on his couch watching television. He was connected to the IV and his wife, Cyndii, was seated next to him. "I was so weak I could hardly move," he says. "I couldn't even dress myself."

The McLains were watching the "Mighty Warrior Conference" that was being broadcast nationally from our church, the Orlando Christian Center. "We began to watch the special telecasts each night as my strength would allow," he says.

Charlie describes what happened. "I watched as Pastor Hinn prayed for people. To be honest, I was a little skeptical because of many of the things I had seen on religious television programs. I wanted to know if what I was seeing was real."

Charlie believed that the Lord had the power to heal, but as he watched the program he said, "God, show me that this is really You. Let me know this is valid; show me there is integrity here."

About that time, as I was ministering during the last few minutes of the program, I spun around to the camera and said, "This is the power of God. Do you want it?"

Charlie, who had already been under the surgeon's knife twice, did not take long to answer. "Yes, Lord," Charlie said, in his weak and helpless condition. "I want it. I need a miracle!"

What happened next was so astounding that the McLains couldn't believe what they were seeing or hearing. As McLain tells it, "Benny turned and looked directly into the camera and said, 'Charlie! Look at me!' Then he continued to pray for the rest of the people who were in the service."

When it happened, Charlie's wife was absolutely stunned. "I felt as though I was almost knocked off the couch," she says.

Charlie was amazed, but he was too weak to respond. "I really didn't feel any unusual sensation," he recalls. "There was no twenty-one gun salute, and the stars didn't fall from heaven. But I knew what happened was more than a coincidence. I took it as a message from the Lord that He was beginning the healing of my intestinal blockage."

Grits and Soft-Boiled Eggs

The next day Charlie and Cyndii looked at each other and he said, "Did Benny Hinn really say that?" Fortunately, they had videotaped the program, and they played that section again. There it was: "Charlie! Look at me!"

Cyndii said, "Honey, I believe you are healed."

She went to the kitchen and cooked dinner. Charlie ate some mashed potatoes—his first solid food since December. "Then on Sunday morning I ate some grits and some soft-boiled eggs," he says.

What happened on Monday? Charlie says, "There is only one evidence that your intestinal tract is working and Cyndii heard me screaming in the bathroom. 'I'm healed! I'm healed!'"

Charlie had the physical evidence to know that he was really healed.

That week some of McLain's friends who had

prayed for him in the hospital saw him. They couldn't believe their eyes. "We were at a Mexican restaurant and I was eating fajitas," he smiles. "The next day we had Chinese food."

Then he went to the office of the gastro-enterologist who had treated him for several months—the one who had told him what a lengthy ordeal he faced.

"Well, how are you doing today?" he asked, surprised to see Charlie walking on his own.

Charlie told him, "It looks like I'm healed."

The doctor said, "Sure you are. What have you been doing?"

"Well, I had a couple of soft-boiled eggs," McLain responded.

The doctor said, "That's very good. That's smart."

Then Charlie added, "The fajitas were really good, too. And I really enjoyed the Chinese food."

As the examination continued, the doctor became more and more convinced that something had truly happened to Charlie. Further testing revealed that the intestine was clear. The doctor said, "You know, it surely wasn't anything we did!"

The *Tulsa World* documented McLain's healing in a major feature article. "There are a lot of things in medicine you just can't explain," one of his doctors said.

Ten Thousand Charlies

Charlie McLain believes the Lord honors the faith of those who look to Him for healing. "For quite some time after my miracle I wondered why the words I heard were, 'Charlie! Look at me!' rather than 'Listen to me!'" he says. "I realized, however, that it was not Benny Hinn who was talking to me, but the Lord. He was telling me, 'Don't look at the circumstances and fail to believe.' Jesus was saying, 'Put your trust in God. Look at me.'"

As Charlie says, "There may be ten thousand Charlies out there who were sick and got healed that night, but I feel God spoke to me by His testimony and by the blood of the Lamb." He adds, "There were those who thought it was a coincidence, but there were too many coincidences for it to be anything but a miracle."

Says McLain, "When man couldn't help me, God did."

Chapter 23

---†---

It Happened in a Flash

Back in Illinois, nurse Sarah Knapp was still in agony because surgery could not correct her problem of thoracic outlet syndrome. Doctors said it was caused by years of lifting patients and moving heavy medical equipment. "The nerves were still pinched and the torment in my arm and shoulder was almost unbearable," she says.

For quite some time the Knapps had watched our ministry on television. When they heard that we had scheduled a crusade in Spartanburg, South Carolina, they decided to attend. It was March 1991.

Even though the event was a great distance from their home in southern Illinois, Sarah told her husband, Don, "If I can just get over there, I know I will be healed."

The journey was one of anticipation and excitement. "We had never attended one of Pastor Hinn's crusades."

The auditorium was much too small and hundreds were turned away. But somehow the Knapps were able to find a seat.

Sarah's faith was so strong that she did not have to wait for the moment in the service when I prayed for the sick and afflicted. Sarah recalls what happened during the song service. "My arm began to vibrate like it had been charged with electricity. Then, in a flash, my shoulder and my arm seemed to open up. The pain vanished," she says.

Back to the Doctor

The trip home seemed short. The Knapps were praising the Lord every mile of the way. "Even though the pain and suffering had gone from my arm and shoulder, it took a couple of weeks for the muscle to return to my forearm," she says. "All of my friends found out what had happened and they were thrilled for me."

Most important, she went back to her doctor in Marion, Illinois, for an examination. His report says, "Sarah Knapp is a patient we have been following over the last several years. The condition was thoracic outlet syndrome. She has had a bilateral first rib resection and bilateral scalene anticus decompressions."

The report continued, "She had chronic pain in her forearms and numbness in her forearms and weakness in both of her forearms until recently when she attended a crusade at Spartanburg, South Carolina, and now is miraculously cured. She has a normal neurological examination and is asymptomatic. She has already assumed a job at a nursing home in West Frankfort. She'll be discharged and seen back as needed."

Sarah thanks God every day for her miracle.

Chapter 24

————— † —————

Timothy's Transformation

Timothy Mercer, the infant who was born prematurely with hypoplastic lungs and a severe kidney problem, was not responding to medical treatment. He had been in and out of Orlando, Florida, hospitals since he was born.

His mother, Wanda, did not know where to turn for an answer. Ann, the baby's grandmother, had begun to attend services at our church, the Orlando Christian Center. She was introduced to a man in our congregation who was part of the hospital visitation team. When he learned of her grandson's condition he gave her a card with his phone number on it.

A few days later, toward the end of October 1990, Timothy was back in the hospital with respiratory failure. Ann dialed the number on the card and said,

"Sir, I need you to pray. They're going to put Timothy back on the respirator."

The man she called told her, "No, they're not. I'm going to meet you at the hospital, and we are going to pray that God will stabilize him so that he can return home."

Soul Searching

Ann Mercer wasn't raised in a church that believed in miracles. This was all quite new to their family. "I didn't know what to think," she recalls.

At the hospital the man prayed and said, "You are going to see a definite change in Timothy tomorrow. And when you bring him home we are going to take him to church and have Pastor Benny lay hands on him and pray that the Lord will perform a total miracle."

When Timothy was born, his grandmother was doing some serious soul searching. "I wasn't serving God at that time," she says. "None of my family was. I was raised in church, but when I moved away from home I stopped attending the house of the Lord and forgot about God." That's the way it had been for twenty years.

Waiting outside a hospital room with her grandson's life in the balance, she remembered how to call on God. "I made an altar right there and asked the Lord to come into my heart. I also made some solemn promises to Him," she says.

Ann told God that if He would bring little Timothy back to health and stabilize him, she would never smoke again, and would serve Him for the rest of her life. She says, "I threw my cigarettes in the trash can just to prove I was serious."

Now Timothy was again fighting for his life.

The next morning the doctor phoned. He said he didn't know what had happened, but Timothy was improving and perhaps could go home in a few days.

The family took him home on November 8, 1990. "The doctor said that if Timothy went into respiratory failure once more, he would die because his lungs just were not growing," his grandmother says. "Even our friends were pessimistic after what the baby had been through. They said, 'Prepare yourself; he probably won't make it.'"

Ann prayed, "Lord, I have to put my trust in You because we have nowhere else to turn. I need to know that You are real in my life and in this baby's life."

That night she also had to answer some tough questions. She thought. "Am I going to serve God, even if the Lord takes Timothy from us? Could I still believe in God if He didn't heal my grandson?"

It seemed that a battle was raging in the Mercer household all day on Sunday, November 11, 1990. Ann finally came to the place where she made a total commitment to the Lord. She said, "If you choose to take my grandson home, I will still serve You."

That night they brought little Timothy to church. The grandmother knew that if God was real she had nothing to lose and everything to gain. They were seated in the back of the auditorium. Her friend said, "I don't know how it is going to happen, but

Pastor Benny is going to lay hands on this baby tonight."

A Brightened Face

In the middle of the service that evening, I felt led to ask several people in the back of the auditorium to come to the platform for healing. Ann Mercer brought little Timothy forward. At the age of four months, he weighed only eight pounds.

My prayer for that baby was, "Father God, in Jesus' name, let the anointing of God flow through this child. Bring healing and deliverance right now in Jesus' name. Perfect healing."

Then I said, "Look, the child is responding!" When I touched the little boy, his face just brightened up. "Lady, take that child back to the doctor. There's been a miracle."

"When Pastor Hinn laid his hands on our baby," she states, "a heat hit Timothy, and I could feel it spread through me. It didn't go away until the next day."

On Monday morning they took him back to the physician. It was obvious that a miracle had begun. They even started his immunization shots, which previously he had been too sick to take.

Within one month Timothy's weight had doubled, and he was taken off oxygen and the heart monitor. The doctors released him because they could not find anything wrong with him.

That was tremendous progress for a child about whom one doctor said, "Even if he lives, he is not going to be like other babies because he lost so much oxygen."

On his first birthday, his grandmother took him back to visit the doctor. "He told me that Timothy was the sickest baby he had ever put on an Extra Corporeal Membrane Oxygenation (ECMO) unit who had lived," says Ann. "His lungs began to develop and he no longer needed to be on oxygen. He is able to participate in activities normal for his age. It's nothing short of a miracle." They ran every test possible and couldn't find anything wrong with him. They were concerned about his speech development, but he learned to say "Praise God."

Through Timothy's healing, almost every member of the Mercer family has accepted Christ as personal Savior and is serving Him. Says Ann, "I am so thankful to the Lord for giving me back my grandson, for picking our family out of the pit we were in, and planting our feet on the solid rock."

The December 18, 1990, report from the Orlando Regional Medical Center included three words that caused the Mercer family to stop again and praise the Lord. It said, "Baby doing well."

Chapter 25

———— † ————

The End of the Road

What was Doreen Maddeaux to do? Since being diagnosed with coronary artery disease in 1987, she had already undergone bypass surgery. Now this.

In July 1992 she was back in the heart ward of a Toronto hospital in a life–and–death situation. She told the doctors, "I didn't say I'm not going to have the operation, but you have to give me three weeks."

That's when the doctor asked, "What do you want three weeks for?"

She replied, "Because I've got to talk to God. I can't die before I talk to God."

He said, "Talk to God here."

Doreen told him, "I can't. I've got to get out."

As she describes it, "When you are surrounded by so much doubt, you have to make a decision. And I believed with all my heart that God was going to heal me."

The heart patient knew exactly what she was going to do.

One night Doreen was seated in the hallway of the hospital reading my book *The Anointing.* She read the question, "How much can I trust you with?"

"What do you mean, 'Trust me'?" she asked the Lord.

The Lord spoke to her and said, "Are you willing to leave this hospital in the condition you are in and take a step of faith?" He said, "You take the first step, and I'll take the second."

At that moment she said, "I'll do it."

"That's Me!"

Doreen turned on a television set at the medical center, and one of our programs was on. She heard me say these words: "There is a lady in the hospital who has been told she has to have an operation. She has learned there is no hope for her either way." And she heard me say these final words. "Honey, you are not going to die; you are going to live."

Doreen moved to the edge of her chair and said, "That's me! That's me!"

For many years she had followed our ministry and was a regular viewer of our television program in Canada. Now she felt that if somehow she could get to one of our crusades she would be healed.

"I knew that Benny Hinn would be conducting meetings in Toronto in September, but that was too long to wait," she says. "The doctors were telling me I wouldn't last that long."

One of our crusades was scheduled the last week of July in Lansing, Michigan. "I made up my mind

that no matter what it took, I was going to be there,"
she said. "My situation was desperate. I had come
to the end of the road."

It was the first time in her entire life that Doreen
had to take such a giant step of faith.

After much discussion, the doctors allowed her to
be transferred to her home and arranged for constant nursing care and supervision. She was given
two containers of oxygen—a small one for traveling
to and from the hospital and a large one to be placed
next to her bed. "It looked like a huge bomb," she
says.

When a group of Christians came to pray for her,
Doreen told them her secret. "I'm going to Lansing," she said.

They couldn't believe her. "Why don't you wait
and go to the meetings here in September?" they
asked. "And who will take you? It sounds impossible."

"You don't understand," she replied. "I don't have
many days left. Something must happen now. If I
have to take this bed and go alone, I'll be in Lansing!"

Doreen thought to herself, "Why are you saying
all of this? How are you going to get there?" Then
suddenly a Jewish friend came for a visit. She told
him of her overwhelming desire.

"Is this really what you want?" he asked. Then
Doreen heard him on the telephone in another
room say, "How do I get a sick woman to Lansing,
Michigan?" He called travel agencies, bus stations,
air ambulance companies, and the train station.

At that instant Doreen knew she was going.

A Secret Journey

Doreen's first problem was the nurses. "How am I going to get rid of them?" she wondered. Would they consent for her to be alone? She told them, "I have decided to go out of town for a couple of days. I need a break from being sick."

The nurses phoned the doctor and said, "Doreen is asking to get away. She is getting overwrought with this problem and just wants a break for a few days. What do you think?"

The doctor told them, "She can go provided she takes a wheelchair."

The nurses arranged for the chair, but they had no idea that within a few hours Doreen would be on a train bound for Michigan.

"My friend had ordered three tickets," she says. "He wasn't going, but two other friends decided to join me. They were the same ones who had earlier cautioned me about the trip." It was a direct route from Toronto to Lansing.

On July 23, 1992, Doreen and her friends went to the station. With the help of an electric lift, she boarded the train. The oxygen tank was placed just behind her.

"The moment the train started moving, I felt something begin to happen," she says. "Suddenly I began to breathe without the use of oxygen. The Lord had already started His work on me."

Their hotel in Lansing was across the street from the train station and just one block from Breslin Center where the services were scheduled.

"What's the Problem?"

On the first night of the crusade, Doreen was seated in a special wheelchair section. She arrived at 2:00 P.M. and was there until the end of the service. "I spent most of the time trying to encourage those who were near me. Although my faith was strong, nothing seemed to be happening," she says.

Late that night, when Doreen returned to her room, the phone was ringing with emergency calls.

"What's the problem?" Doreen asked her Jewish friend on the other end of the line.

"They are blaming me because you left town," he said with great concern. Her sister, and even her doctors, had learned about the nature of her trip and were upset. They did not believe in miracles.

When she returned a phone call to her daughter, Doreen was devastated. "She couldn't understand how I could do such a thing, and she hung up on me," Doreen says. "I thought my heart would break, and I cried myself to sleep."

On Friday morning Doreen returned to the crusade for a special anointing service. "Seated in my wheelchair in the balcony, my eyes were still filled with tears," she says. "My spirit was broken because of my physical condition and because of my family."

As the service progressed, one of the soloists began to sing the familiar words, "His eye is on the sparrow, and I know He watches me." Doreen felt the song was just for her.

What happened next was something she could hardly believe. As Doreen recalls, "Benny said,

'Someone in the balcony was just healed of a serious heart condition while the music was playing.' Then he said, 'I only want those people I call to come forward.'"

Doreen jumped out of her wheelchair and began to run down the stairs with an usher. "At the front of the platform someone asked me to run back and forth and they checked my pulse. My heart rate was normal!"

In the hospital, Doreen's pulse "had dropped to thirty-five and had only come up to fifty-six," she says. Now it was normal.

"I don't remember too much of what happened that Friday morning," says Doreen. "I could feel the power of God all around me." It was like a scene from the book of Acts as she was leaping and praising God. "I only know that God kept His word, and I was healed."

Doreen knew that the Lord had broken the curse of heart disease that had been in her family for generations.

Waiting for Results

On the train back to Toronto, Doreen went from seat to seat to share what God had done for her. "I sent back the wheelchair as baggage," she exclaims. "When I arrived in Toronto I walked from the train and even ran up the ramps at the station."

When Doreen got home, she tried to reach her doctors but learned that they would be on vacation until two days before her operation was scheduled. "I immediately called a cardiologist I had seen before, and he arranged a stress test on August 4, 1992, at

Missisauga Hospital," she says. "He was informed at the hospital of my condition."

That day's results were quite a contrast from the results of tests taken just a few weeks earlier. "The doctor asked to see me in the hall," she recalls. "He said, 'The only thing I can say is that your problem is in remission.'"

Doreen still likes to look at the letter from her surgeon that says, "Arrangements have been made for your admission to the Toronto General Hospital on Tuesday, August 18, 1992, for surgery on Thursday, August 20, 1992."

The surgery was canceled.

On September 17, 1992, her cardiologist sent a report to her physician: "I saw Doreen in the office on September 16. She continues to look absolutely wonderful and is totally asymptomatic. She is walking an hour a day; she is taking only an aspirin a day. She has had virtually no angina and shortness of breath."

The report concluded, "In summary, Doreen presents a modern-day miracle. Several months ago she was unable to exercise for much more than a minute on a treadmill, but as you know, on August 4, 1992, she went for 5:42 (minutes) up to a heart rate of 127, with no ischemic ST changes nor chest pain. She achieved a workload of 7 METS."

Today, Doreen Maddeaux is living a normal, healthy life. "I am doing things again I thought I would never do. I still pause for a second when I see a flight of stairs because I remember how it was—not because I have to."

One of her doctors saw her testimony on a telecast

and said, "When I saw you running up those stairs, I could hardly believe it. I remember when you could barely make it up the stairs to my office."

What about her Jewish friends? "They are astonished at my healing and don't know how to explain it," said Doreen. "I'm a living miracle that our God reigns."

Chapter 26

✝

Celebration of a Miracle

"When you are told that you have thirty—and at the outside ninety—days to live, you begin to put things in perspective," said Dave Lane, from Cookeville, Tennessee.

"Suddenly, my championship Arabian horses didn't mean very much," he says. All he could think about was how he was going to spend the remaining days with his wife and family. His mind could not escape the thought of the dreaded baseball-size cancer that was killing him.

As Dave was walking through the den of his home the day following his diagnosis, the program on his big-screen television caught his eyes. "It was Benny Hinn's *Miracle Invasion* and I felt compelled to stop what I was doing and watch," says Lane. "I had only seen the program once before. But that day it was as if the presence of the Holy Spirit penetrated the set and began to minister to me."

We announced that our crusade team from Orlando would be conducting special services Thursday and Friday of that same week in Rockwall, Texas, near Dallas, at Church on the Rock. That was in June 1990. Says Dave, "I felt God saying 'Go!'—instructing me to drive to Dallas for those services."

Immediately, Dave's mind was filled with doubt. "Is it right that I should take a trip that will take three days out of the thirty the doctors are giving me?" he wondered.

The Road to Rockwall

Like so many Christians, Dave was raised in a church that believed miracles were limited to the time of Christ's ministry on earth. But the more he read Scripture, the more convinced he became that healing was part of the atonement and is for us today.

The first part of that week the doctors continued to call. They knew the urgency of scheduling surgery and could not understand why Dave was avoiding them.

"On Thursday morning my wife and I got in our car and headed for Rockwall," says Lane. "It was about a twelve-hour drive, and we had about thirteen hours to get there." But when they arrived in the area they found it impossible to find a motel with a vacancy. "We had to stop to change clothes several miles away, and we were about an hour late getting to the auditorium."

On the way Dave and Rebecca prayed for three

things. He said, "I asked that the Lord would (1) provide us with a good seat near the front, (2) delay the preaching part of the service until we arrived, and (3) let me be prayed for by the evangelist, so that I would be healed of the cancerous tumor in my body."

When the Lanes arrived there were many people standing around the outside of the building who could not get in. "But for some unknown reason," says Dave, "a gentleman walked up to us and invited us to accompany him inside. He ushered us to two seats near the front of the auditorium that were still unoccupied."

When Dave walked into the crusade, all he could think about was his cancer. "But the moment I got in God's presence and the anointing began to move in that place, things changed," he said. "Just ten minutes in that precious atmosphere was worth all of the effort it took for the long drive to Texas."

That night in Dallas, Dave committed his life totally and completely to the Lord. "I came to realize that even if I died, my death would be just a doorway into eternal life with Christ."

Suddenly Dave got his mind off of his problem and onto Christ. "When I began to praise the Lord, I completely forgot about my cancer," he says. "A heavenly warmth seemed to wash over me."

When I called for those who felt God was healing them to come forward, Dave stepped to the aisle. "I had no physical evidence, but I knew beyond doubt that God had done something awesome inside of me," he said.

Suddenly Dave was ushered to the platform. "Pastor Hinn laid his hands on me and said of the cancer,

'I curse its roots and command it to die,'" recalls Dave. "I knew right then it was leaving my body."

All of his prayers had been answered.

"Was I Healed?"

Dave and his wife returned to Tennessee. Every day he felt stronger and stronger, both physically and spiritually. Thirty days passed, and he was still alive. After ninety days, Dave was still claiming his healing.

"The doctors who initially diagnosed my cancer simply couldn't understand why I continued to ignore their pleas to schedule surgery and begin cancer treatment," says Lane. In October, about four months after the original diagnosis, Dave told his wife, "I'm going to a different doctor for a check-up—someone who doesn't know my problem."

After the uncomfortable proctoscopic exam, the doctor called Dave's wife into the room. "I'm sorry to give you this report," said the physician, "but Mr. Lane, you have a lesion the size of a quarter. And it is malignant."

Dave and Rebecca looked at each other. They were both thinking the same thing—"Praise the Lord!" Then Dave began to smile.

"I'm sure that doctor must have thought I had lost my mind," he said. "But I was excited that a baseball had just been reduced to a quarter. That was a miracle in itself," he says. "Plus, I believe we don't serve a half-way God. What the Lord starts He finishes."

Now there was another doctor calling Dave. "Mr. Lane, we need to do something about this before it gets any larger," he said. Lane placed the matter in God's hands and kept on smiling.

The medical report from the October visit said, "I looked at the lower G.I. tract in the office and biopsied a suspicious area for a possible tumor. The pathology report as described . . . revealed that this was a malignancy showing what was called intramucosal carcinoma. This is a recurrent cancer of the upper portion of the rectum."

The letter continued, "I have had some difficulty getting in touch with you and did want to review this with you and discuss possible options. I am free to discuss this and will be happy to see you at any time. I would, however, like to stress to you that this is a matter of utmost importance and that with the finding of a rectal cancer specific steps need to be taken in order to correct the problem and not allow this to continue to an advanced stage."

"I had asked God to let me know beyond any doubt that I did not have cancer. I felt healthy and strong, but I continued to ask God for the assurance of my healing," Dave says.

"You're Free!"

In March 1992, Dave began feeling ill. "Lord, what is happening? Am I losing my healing?" Lane wondered.

Dave returned to a doctor at the Park View Medical Center in Nashville who knew he had cancer. He asked for a new examination and learned that he had an abscess on his appendix that needed immediate attention.

When they performed surgery, they did a complete exam of Dave's body, including the area where the cancer had been. The most important discovery was what they *didn't* find. "Your body has no cancer in it," the doctors told him.

Dave was rejoicing that the surgery for his appendix proved beyond any doubt that God had completely and totally healed his cancer. Further ultrasound exams showed there were no tumors in his colon.

As he looks back on his experience with cancer, Dave says, "I realize that Benny Hinn had nothing to do with the healing except that the Lord has honored Benny with His presence. It's the Lord who performed the miracle."

Before his healing, "God was something distant," says Lane. "Now I have a personal relationship with the Healer. I know that the Bible says that God will give you the desire of your heart. Now God *is* the desire of my heart."

The report from the medical center in Nashville on March 3, 1992, says,

1. Eight (8) regional mesenteric lymph nodes are free of metastic carcinoma.
2. Additional rectal margin: no evidence of malignancy.
3. Rectal side of anastomosis: negative for malignancy.
4. Colonic site of anastomosis: negative for malignancy.

On April 22, 1992, the same doctor who two years earlier confirmed that he had colon cancer, wrote, "There is no evidence of residual malignancy, and he at this point should be considered free of malignant disease."

Dave Lane had no radiation, no chemotherapy, no colostomy, and no medicine for his cancer. He was totally healed by the power of God.

Afterword

Healing: An Act of Faith

Since the beginning of my ministry, I have heard the testimonies of thousands of people who have received their miracle of healing. Because of our television ministry and large crusades, some people have said, "If only I could have Benny Hinn personally pray for me, I know I would be healed."

But that is not the key to your miracle.

It is God's response to your *faith* that brings healing. Let me illustrate.

Candy Brusseau was born profoundly deaf in both ears. As a child she spent many frustrating years learning to speak a few simple words and phrases. Throughout her adult life she has continued to cope with this handicap.

In mid-1992, Candy was summoned to jury duty by the Los Angeles Superior Court. On November 3,

1992, in response to the summons, her physician, the noted ear surgeon Dr. Howard House, wrote a letter to the judicial court recommending that Candy be excused from jury service. He stated that Candy "has been followed intermittently in this office since 1954, because of a severe hearing impairment." Dr. House further stated that, "Unfortunately, there is no medical or surgical therapy that will restore her hearing."

On October 22, 1992, twelve days prior to Dr. House's letter, Candy and her family—as an act of faith in the finished work of Jesus Christ—joined in composing a simple testimonial for future use; a testimonial of praise and thanksgiving for what they felt certain would be her forthcoming healing by the God with whom all things are possible, and who is not limited to "medical or surgical therapy."

They wrote: "My story is not about being born a profoundly deaf person; though I was born profoundly deaf. It is not about my failed ear fenestration surgery by one of the world's great audiologists and ear surgeons. My story is about the wonderful, miraculous healing of my deafness through the grace of God on December 11, 1992, at a Benny Hinn Miracle Crusade Service at the Long Beach (California) Municipal Arena."

In her deafness, she claimed deliverance.

On Friday night, December 11, over fourteen thousand people jammed the auditorium. At about 5:45 P.M., more than an hour before the service began, wonderful healings were taking place all over the auditorium.

As Mrs. Joan Gieson was passing along the nearby

aisle, Bill Brusseau, Candy's father, requested of Mrs. Gieson that she join in a "prayer of faith" for Candy. At the conclusion of that prayer, there was an audible, spontaneous exclamation of praise from those sitting nearby, as Candy removed her hearing aid, turned to her father, and said "I can hear!"

Later, in a letter to relatives and friends about that Friday evening, December 11, 1992, her mother and father wrote; "The Holy Spirit came upon our dear Candy, and in a most profound and beautiful manner she was miraculously healed of her lifelong deafness."

When she was brought to the platform that night, Candy was aglow with the presence of the Lord. Her testimony was no longer future, it was *now*. Even before I arrived for the service, Candy Brusseau was healed. Her faith had made her whole.

My Prayer For You

It is exciting to hear the stories of those who have been healed by God's power. But what about you? What is your need? Perhaps you are saying, "Lord, I need a miracle!"

Would you allow me to pray for you? Even now, reach out in faith as I call on God for your healing.

Lord, I bless Your name today. You are the God who forgives our iniquities, who heals our diseases, who redeems our life from destruction, and who crowns our life with loving kindness and tender mercies. You are the one who satisfies our mouth with good things, who renews our youth like the eagle's, and who is our defender. Now,

Lord, I pray for a blanket of a healing to cover Your child. Right now, I stand on Your Word and declare instant and total restoration. Do it for Your sake. In Jesus' Name and for Your Glory. Amen.

Claim God's miracle today. His Word was written for you: "By His stripes we are healed" (Isa. 53:5).

The Lord is waiting to hear your praise, your worship, and your celebration. He is waiting to hear you say, "Thank You, Lord, for my miracle."

----------✝----------

If God has given you a miracle of healing as a result of reading this book, I would love to rejoice with you. Please send me your testimony along with a report from your physician that documents what the Lord has done. My address is:

Benny Hinn
Lord, I Need a Miracle
Box 90
Orlando, FL 32802-0090